Addressing Race-Based Stress in Therapy with Black Clients

Despite Black Americans being at high risk for negative mental health symptoms due to racism and other chronic stresses, disparities persist in the provision of mental health services to this population. This book addresses that gap in clinical practice by explicitly calling attention to the experience of race-based stress in the Black community.

Johnson and Melton urge mental health practitioners to action in promoting societal understanding, affirmation, and appreciation of multiculturalism against the damaging effects of individual, institutional, and societal racism, prejudice, and all forms of oppression based on stereotyping and discrimination. Chapters include worksheets, vignettes, and case studies to provide a practical framework for implementing an effective, nonpathological approach to ameliorating the damaging effects of race-based trauma and stress.

This book will give tools and strategies for mental health professionals to responsibly use scientific and professional knowledge to improve the condition of individuals, communities, and, by extension, society.

Monica M. Johnson, PsyD, is a clinical psychologist and owner of Kind Mind Psychology in New York City. Her practice focuses on treating individuals from marginalized groups, and she specializes in CBT and DBT interventions. Her professional interests focus on work with multiculturalism, appropriate adaptation of evidence-based practices, and supervision and training.

Michelle L. Melton, PsyD, is a clinical psychologist offering consultation and clinical services in Phoenix, AZ. She has been published in state and national scholarly journals. H̲e̲r̲ ̲ ̲ ̲ ̲ ̲ ̲l̲ interests include supervision and t̲ ̲ ̲ ̲ ̲ ̲ development, and multiculturalism

Addressing Race-Based Stress in Therapy with Black Clients

Using Multicultural and Dialectical Behavior Therapy Techniques

Monica M. Johnson
Michelle L. Melton

Routledge
Taylor & Francis Group
NEW YORK AND LONDON

First published 2021
by Routledge
52 Vanderbilt Avenue, New York, NY 10017

and by Routledge
2 Park Square, Milton Park, Abingdon, Oxon, OX14 4RN

Routledge is an imprint of the Taylor & Francis Group, an informa business

© 2021 Taylor & Francis

The right of Monica M. Johnson and Michelle L. Melton to be identified as authors of this work has been asserted by them in accordance with sections 77 and 78 of the Copyright, Designs and Patents Act 1988.

All rights reserved. The purchase of this copyright material confers the right on the purchasing institution to photocopy pages which bear the photocopy icon and copyright line at the bottom of the page. No other part of this publication may be reproduced, stored in a retrieval system, or transmitted in any form or by any means, electronic, mechanical, photocopying, recording or otherwise, without prior permission in writing from the publishers.

Trademark notice: Product or corporate names may be trademarks or registered trademarks, and are used only for identification and explanation without intent to infringe.

Library of Congress Cataloging-in-Publication Data
Names: Johnson, Monica M., author. | Melton, Michelle L., author.
Title: Addressing race-based stress in therapy with black clients : using multicultural and dialectical behavior therapy techniques / Monica M. Johnson, Michelle L. Melton.
Description: New York, NY : Routledge, 2020. | Includes bibliographical references and index. | Identifiers: LCCN 2020011479 (print) | LCCN 2020011480 (ebook) | ISBN 9781138339521 (hardback) | ISBN 9781138339538 (paperback) | ISBN 9780429441059 (ebook)
Subjects: MESH: African Americans–psychology | Stress, Psychological–therapy | Behavior Therapy | Cultural Competency | Race Factors | United States Classification: LCC RC451.5.N4 (print) | LCC RC451.5.N4 (ebook) | NLM WA 305 AA1 | DDC 616.890089/96073–dc23
LC record available at https://lccn.loc.gov/2020011479
LC ebook record available at https://lccn.loc.gov/2020011480

ISBN: 978-1-138-33952-1 (hbk)
ISBN: 978-1-138-33953-8 (pbk)
ISBN: 978-0-429-44105-9 (ebk)

Typeset in Palatino
by Swales & Willis, Exeter, Devon, UK

Visit the eResources: https://www.routledge.com/9781138339538

Contents

List of Illustrations — vii

Preface — ix

Acknowledgments — xi

Part I. Foundational Knowledge — 1

Chapter 1   Components of Cultural Competence — 3

Chapter 2   Re-envisioning Ethics Through a Multicultural-Oriented Framework — 27

Chapter 3   Advocacy and Consultation Regarding Race-Based Stress — 47

Part II. Implementing Culturally Responsive Care — 63

Chapter 4   Assessment and Diagnosis of Race-Based Stress — 65

Chapter 5   Engaging in Race Talk and Addressing Microaggressions in Therapy — 85

| Chapter 6 | Culturally Responsive Interventions | 115 |

References 201

Index 211

Illustrations

Figure

3.1	Model of Change Through Resilience and Empowerment	50

Tables

1.1	ADDRESSING Framework	11
1.2	ADDRESSING Framework – Case Example	12
3.1	Model of Change Through Resilience and Empowerment	51
3.2	Sample Advocacy Plan	59

Preface

We hope this book can serve as a practical manual for concepts and strategies to keep in mind when working with this population on issues related to their race-based trauma. Unfortunately, we live in a time when marginalized groups are being targeted and so those of us in helping professions need to be ready to address the consequences of the sociopolitical climate. In our own practices on nearly a daily basis we receive calls and emails from individuals within these groups (e.g. people of color, LGBTQ, women) that are specifically seeking care and guidance to better cope with their own oppression. We have chosen to focus on Black Americans, but understand that much of what we cover can be applicable to other groups. We believe this is important for specificity and we hope that others will follow in kind as often having one chapter dedicated to a group is not enough. In the literature you will find many definitions for race-based stress or race-based trauma or race-based traumatic stress, however, we have used these terms interchangeably throughout the text and have chosen to use the acronym RBS. Additionally, there are variations in definition and for the purposes of this text we have chosen to use Carter's (2007) definition, which will be discussed at greater length in the text. In general, RBS is an adverse response to experiences of racism. In moving forward, we hope that you will remember to BE REAL in your work with marginalized groups:

acknowledge **B**iases and **B**lind Spots
Evaluate racial identity and acculturation
Respect cultural values, perspectives, and strengths
Employ empathy
make **A**mends when necessary
Liberate through fostering resilience and empowerment through culturally appropriate interventions

What This Book Is Not: it is not an exhaustive exploration of the concepts discussed. Frankly, if you want to do this work, you have to do the work. We hope that you will continue to read books and articles, attend conferences, and engage in cultural activities that are representative of yourself and the populations that you serve. Finally, none of the case illustrations in this book is of real people – each is a composite.

Acknowledgments

For my mother, Rose Davis, who taught me how to be strong in all the ways that she was and all the ways that she pretended to be. For Aunt Julia Singh who allowed me to fully express myself as a Black woman. For my brother, Anthony Carraway who was my male role model as a child and never left me behind. Finally, for my husband David Moore for his unending support, dedication, and love. I am eternally grateful for the support of these individuals and the wonderful friendships I have fostered in my life.

Monica M. Johnson

I must first honor my mother, Beatrice Antoinette Johnson Melton, who first taught me how to speak truth to power. For my sister, Lisa Melton, who has been my greatest encourager and champion. For my father, Louis Melton, for helping me to remember the laughter and resilience in our story. I am equally grateful to the following family, friends, and colleagues for their encouragement, support, and suggestions: Stefan (PA) Harris, Leo Caraballo, Louise Baca, Kelli Johnson, Greg Shrader, Laurel Reed, and Teresa Imholte.

Michelle L. Melton

PART I
Foundational Knowledge

Chapter 1	Components of Cultural Competence	3
Chapter 2	Re-envisioning Ethics Through a Multicultural-Oriented Framework	27
Chapter 3	Advocacy and Consultation Regarding Race-Based Stress	47

CHAPTER 1
Components of Cultural Competence

Adopting a Multicultural Orientation

Within psychotherapy communities increased attention has been given to the importance of a multicultural orientation (MCO). Much is owed to Sue et al.'s (1982) tripartite model of multicultural competencies that consists of three components: attitudes/beliefs, knowledge, and skills. The model asserts that therapists' awareness of their own cultural background, attitudes and beliefs, knowledge of diverse clients' worldviews, and use of culturally appropriate skills are the foundation of developing competency. Additional research has been conducted since that time that seeks to provide more contextualization to addressing multicultural concerns in the therapy room. Owen et al. (2011) introduced the multicultural orientation framework as a way to better conceptualize and define the variables that arise within therapists' culturally focused interventions in session. The multicultural orientation framework consists of three components: cultural humility, cultural opportunities, and cultural comfort (Hook, Davis, Owen, Worthington, & Utsey, 2013, Hook et al., 2017; Tervalon & Murray-Garcia, 1998), which will be discussed in more detail later. Research supports that several race-related variables affect the mental and physical health of Black Americans (Harrell, Hall, & Taliaferro, 2003; Pieterse & Carter, 2007). Given this knowledge and the focus of this text to address race-based stress (RBS), we believe that adopting an ethnopolitical approach, as discussed by Comas-Díaz (2000), in combination with MCO is important. An ethnopolitical approach is one that recognizes the impact of oppression, racism, and political repression. Comas-Díaz (2000) argued that therapists must take an anti-racist stance in their work with people of color. An anti-racist stance is one in which the therapist does not minimize, ignore, or intellectualize racism. We utilize this orientation with the purpose of opening a space for Black clients to liberate themselves from the negative effects of racial oppression. Regardless of the terms (e.g. cultural sensitivity, humility, competence, etc.) one uses to convey their approach, to truly work with diverse populations takes continual education and self-assessment. If you share diversity variables with the populations that you are treating it does not remove this requirement.

Assumptions of Multicultural Orientation

1. **We assume that therapists and clients co-created cultural expression within therapy** (Hook et al., 2017). As such the therapist can influence the cultural safety felt in the environment. They also have an impact on which cultural identities are more or less prominent to the client. Finally, therapists impact how much cultural heritage is integrated in the therapeutic process (Hook et al., 2017). Consequently, we encourage you to be explicit about the need for and safety of cultural expression early in treatment. It is also imperative to remain aware of the intersectional identities. Typically, multiple factors play a role in culture and identity (e.g. gender, sexuality, religion, etc.) outside of race. All of these identities form the client's unique perspective and experience and should be honored and addressed in treatment. Your cultural identities may influence what you are aware of and have a tendency to highlight. For instance, an Asian, male, secular therapist may underestimate the role of religion for the client. While this text focuses on race-based traumatic stress, the multicultural orientation

is the foundation for all that we do and leaves room to address the whole person.

2. **We assume that multicultural orientation involves a way of being with clients rather than a way of doing therapy** (Owen, 2013; Owen et al., 2011). Owen et al. posit that the multicultural orientation framework is more about the therapist's values regarding culture and the integration of those values throughout the therapy. The actual interventions that are implemented are secondary. Values consistent with the multicultural orientation framework involve being genuine and authentic in engaging in conversations about culture. We feel that this value system, in combination with adapting therapeutic tools to address the psychological impact of race-based stress, can be beneficial to clients.

3. **We assume that cultural processes (e.g. cultural humility) are especially important for connecting with the client's most salient cultural identities: feeling deeply known and accepted sets the stage for effective therapy** (Hook et al., 2017). Talking about the race and the impacts of living in a society that marginalizes those based on race and other variables requires openness, vulnerability, and trust. If the therapist is unable to display humility, the opportunity to effect change may be lost. It is imperative as the therapist that you engage in self-reflection and consult with colleagues that you trust in order to maintain the humility necessary for this work.

4. **We assume that having a strong multicultural orientation motivates therapists to learn new things about their own and their clients' cultural perspectives and worldviews** (Hook et al., 2017). This includes understanding your own limits and seeking out experiences that allow you to learn more about diverse cultures. We have a tendency to surround ourselves with people and things that are similar, likeminded, and support our worldview. It is important to engage with stimuli that challenge us and force us to grow. When is the last time you watched a foreign film or

documentary that was about a group of people that were dissimilar to you? How diverse is your network of friends and colleagues? How proactive are you in seeking out experiences that expand your perspective?

Critical Concepts of a Multicultural Orientation

Cultural humility is the foundational concept that underlies both cultural opportunities and cultural comfort. It is a lifelong process that involves self-reflection, self-critique, and examination of one's own assumptions, biases, and beliefs (Tervalon & Murray-Garcia, 1998). At the same time, culturally humble therapists maintain an other-oriented approach that involves respect and lack of superiority toward other's perspectives and values, etc. There are both intrapersonal and interpersonal aspects of cultural humility. The intrapersonal aspect encompasses how therapists view themselves culturally including their biases, strengths, areas for growth, world view, etc. A key component of the culturally humble therapist is a nondefensive, open stance that allows them to take in feedback and incorporate it to improve their approach and broaden awareness. The interpersonal aspect of cultural humility describes a way of being curious and open toward other's cultural beliefs, rather than being ethnocentric.

Cultural opportunities are moments in therapy in which a client's cultural beliefs, values, or other aspects of cultural identity can be explored (Hook et al., 2017). Each session provides numerous occasions in which culture can be explored and integrated into the process. However, they often go unnoticed because the therapist is not attuned or is fearful of approaching these topics. Sometimes these missed opportunities take the form of microaggressions. Thinking about a missed opportunity, or unintentionally engaging in a microaggression can cause anxiety for a therapist. It is important to remember that perfection is neither expected nor required. Cultural humility and cultural opportunities work in concert with each other. For instance, missed cultural opportunities can lead to poorer treatment outcomes, but these negative effects can be mitigated if the therapist is perceived as being high in cultural humility (Owen et al., 2016). Moreover, microaggressions cause harm to therapeutic alliance, but when therapists address them in session, the alliance can recover to pre-existing levels. The goal is to display a willingness to challenge your biases, build awareness of yourself and others, fine tune your skill set to reduce missteps, and repair when mistakes inevitably occur.

Cultural comfort relates to the therapist's emotional state before, during, and after culturally relevant conversations. We find that many therapists have a tendency to avoid cultural topics due to their discomfort. We want to validate that addressing cultural aspects of others can feel awkward or tense and we encourage you to explore those feelings with the intent of acting opposite. Owen et al. (2017) found that therapists who were less culturally comfortable with racial and ethnic minority (REM) clients had a higher rate of dropout for their REM clients than their White clients. As with any type of exposure, the more you engage with the stimulus that causes fear, the more comfort you gain over time. The goal with cultural comfort is to have feelings of calm, openness, ease, and relaxation. As an example, review the dialog below between Dr. Banach and her client Jennifer, a 32-year-old African American and Mexican female.

Jennifer: I found out a few days ago that I'm pregnant and I'm super anxious and I don't know what to do about it. I'm not in a relationship with the dad and he doesn't want anything to do with the situation. I don't know that I can raise a child by myself. I've tried to pray about it, but I'm not getting any answers.

Dr. Banach: This seems to be causing you a lot of stress and confusion.

Jennifer: Yes, it is.

Dr. Banach: You mentioned anxiety, how has it been affecting you?

Jennifer: I can't sleep because I keep thinking about what I should do? Should I have the baby? Should I have an abortion? Should I give it up for adoption? I know I can't give it up for adoption, if I carry the baby for nine months and see its face, I'll never be able to give it away, but I just know I'll be a terrible mom right now.

8 Foundational Knowledge

Dr. Banach: It is a tough decision and one that requires a lot of thought which is difficult to do if we haven't been sleeping or taking care of ourselves due to anxiety. Let's review some ways to better manage your anxiety so you can have a clear head when approaching this situation.

Jennifer: okay

> **Reflection Point**
>
> In this dialog, Dr. Banach was symptom focused and targeted managing her sleep disturbance brought on by anxiety. In what ways do you think Dr. Banach was helpful? In what ways could she have been harmful or missed opportunities?

Now let's look at the same situation with a different approach.

Jennifer: I found out a few days ago that I'm pregnant and I'm super anxious and I don't know what to do about it. I'm not in a relationship with the dad and he doesn't want anything to do with the situation. I don't know that I can raise a child by myself. I've tried to pray about it, but I'm not getting any answers.

Dr. Banach: This seems to be causing you a lot of stress and confusion.

Jennifer: Yes, it is.

Dr. Banach: You mentioned praying about it. What are the questions you are seeking answers to?

Jennifer: Well, I've been thinking about abortion. I'm Catholic and I know it's a sin, but so is premarital sex and I just don't know what to do!

Dr. Banach: I can see why this is causing you so much conflict. I know that your religion is important to you. Can you tell me a bit about your personal thoughts on abortion?

Jennifer: I do believe in a woman's right to choose. I don't have any negative thoughts about other people making that choice. One of my best friends had an abortion, and I completely support her choice. It's just so hard for me emotionally. I am not in a financial situation where I can support a child. I just got off my friend's couch and into an apartment with roommates two months ago. I've also considered adoption, but I know myself and if I see the baby's face, I am not giving it up.

Dr. Banach: I know in the past we've done pros and cons to help us make decisions and while it may help us with this as well, it appears important to really explore all the variables. Have you thought about speaking to your priest and maybe your friend about this?

Jennifer: I hadn't thought about that. Once I got rejected by the dad, I stayed in panic mode. I have an idea about what each of them will say, but I think hearing it will help me to make a better decision about where I land on this issue.

Reflection Point

In this dialog, Dr. Banach was more culturally focused and targeted Jennifer's religious conflict. In what ways do you think Dr. Banach was helpful? In what ways could she have been harmful or missed opportunities?

Interpersonal Awareness for a Multicultural Orientation

Many researchers and therapists reference the need for both intrapersonal (e.g. self-awareness) and interpersonal (e.g. knowledge of others) aspects that are necessary in order to be an effective multicultural therapist (Hook et al., 2017; Sue et al., 1982). Having a deep awareness of your cultural identities and how these identities are connected with your experiences of privilege and oppression can be vital in the therapy room. When you are working with individuals who are experiencing race-based stress it is crucial to understand how your identities as the therapist may overlap, clash, and overall interact with those of the client. If we are unaware, it can lead to defensiveness, missed cultural opportunities, and blind spots on the part of the therapist. With this context, we recommend the ADDRESSING model to increase your awareness of yourself as a cultural being.

The ADDRESSING framework developed by Hays (2001) can be helpful in reflecting on our own culture (see Table 1.1). It can open us up to begin exploring our cultural history, values, and influences. Moreover, we can begin to confront the ways in which we are oppressed and privileged, as well as how the elements may be affecting our world view and how our clients perceive us in the session. For instance, imagine that you are a therapist working with the homeless population. You are astutely aware of your privilege as it relates to socioeconomic status. You may have even grown up in an economically depressed environment. However, due to your education and level of employment, you are now considered to be middle class. When working with homeless clients you are aware of the need for appropriate therapeutic suggestions made when implementing interventions. For instance, when using behavioral activation for depression, it would be insensitive to recommend obtaining a gym membership or going out to dinner and a movie. Instead, you may spend considerable time working closely with case management to be aware of resources that were available and to have a clear picture of your clients' daily lives. In doing this extra work, you would be able to make suggestions that are realistic and sensitive to the realities of your clients' lives.

The framework is also useful for learning more about our clients by aiding us in developing hypotheses and questions related to their cultural identity. It is important to note that in some cases it may be inappropriate to ask a question directly and could potentially lead to a therapeutic breach if we put our clients in a position of educating us about topics related to their culture on a regular basis. Ultimately, it is our job as therapists to have a general knowledge about the cultures that we are treating in

Table 1.1 ADDRESSING Framework

Cultural Influence	Dominant Group	Non-Dominant Group
Age and generational influences	Young and middle-aged adults	Children, older adults
Developmental or other **D**isability	Nondisabled people	People with cognitive, intellectual, sensory, physical, and psychiatric disabilities
Religious and spiritual orientation	Christian and secular	Muslim, Jews, Hindus, Buddhists, and other religions
Ethnic and racial identity	European Americans	Asian, South Asian, Latinx, Pacific Islander, African, Arab, African American, Middle Eastern, and multiracial people
Socioeconomic status	Upper and middle class	People of lower status by occupation, education, income, or inner city/rural habitats
Sexual orientation	Heterosexuals	People who identify as gay, lesbian, bisexual, or asexual
Indigenous heritage	European Americans	American Indians, Inuit, Alaska Natives, Métis, Native Hawaiians, New Zealand Māori, Aboriginal Australians
National origin	US-born Americans	Immigrants, refugees, and international students
Gender	Men	Women and people who identify as transgender or non-binary

Hays, 2001

Table 1.2 ADDRESSING Framework – Case Example

Cultural Influence	Dominant Group	Non-Dominant Group
Age and generational influences	32 years old, Millennial generation, grew up with the internet, was able to vote for the first African American president	
Developmental or other **D**isability	No developmental or physical disabilities	
Religious and spiritual orientation	Christian, specifically go to a Unitarian church	
Ethnic and racial identity	White, specifically Polish, parents immigrated to America, I am US born and bilingual in Polish and English; however, I consider my primary language to be English	
Socioeconomic status	I currently have a PhD in Clinical Psychology and work as a Psychologist and would consider myself to be middle class	I grew up in a working class immigrant household. Mother worked part time cleaning houses and my father worked at a factory
Sexual orientation		I am a lesbian, currently in long-term relationship of three years
Indigenous heritage	No indigenous background	
National origin	I am US citizen, however, was raised by immigrant parents and am well aware of their experience and how it differs from my own	
Gender		Female

our practices. This allows us to focus our interventions with our clients on learning more about their individual identities within those cultures. For example, a White therapist asking a Black female client, "what do you mean by natural hair?" could be off putting to the client or display an overall lack of knowledge about the population. Natural hair is a major topic within the Black community, especially for women. Whereas, asking questions related to their decision to go natural, what it means to them, and the support or lack thereof that they received, could give you a deeper understanding of the person and strengthen your relationship.

Using the ADDRESSING model, define the areas in which you are of the dominant and non-dominant groups. Please note that some of these areas can change over time. For instance, you may have grown up in a highly religious family, but don't identify with any particular religion at this time. It is important to note both and put a check mark next to the one that reflects your current status. These changes are also important to the shaping of our identity and world view. Table 1.2 has an example of how this may look using the fictional therapist Ewelina Banach.

Using Worksheet 1.1, at the end of this chapter, identify your dimensions of diversity. After completing your ADDRESSING chart, reflect on the following questions:

- How have my areas of privilege shaped me?
- How have my areas of marginalization shaped me?
- What views do I have of others who share my privilege? What views do I have of people who have areas of privilege that I don't?
- What views do I have of others who share my marginalization? What views do I have of people who have areas of marginalization that I don't?
- For those that are marginalized in a similar context, but different, do I view their struggle as different? If so, in what ways? For instance, if I am Black, do I view the struggles of someone who is Asian as different from my own? If I am

gay, do I view the struggles of someone who is bisexual as different from my own?
- Do I ever try to quantify different areas of privilege or marginalization as better or worse than another? If so where do these thoughts/feelings originate?

Understanding of Racial Identity Development in Therapy

As previously stated, adopting a multicultural orientation requires knowledge of self as a cultural being as well as knowledge of others' cultural lived experiences. When addressing race-based stress, it is essential to have foundational awareness of the sociohistorical and sociopolitical history of race and racism in America. Inherent in this knowledge of race and racism is recognition that the group historically or currently defined as White is advantaged, and groups historically or currently defined as non-White (African, Asian, Hispanic, Native American, etc.) are disadvantaged. Furthermore, the ability to recognize racism is dependent on an individual's racial identity development. Consequently, an individual's awareness of race is an important factor in understanding and evaluating raced-based trauma (Carter et al., 2017). This means that accurately assessing racial identity is paramount in conducting treatment focused on RBS as it can affect how the person presents in the room and the level of distress that they may be experiencing. As the therapist, it is important for you to accurately assess yourself as well to reduce the effects of potential biases. We will provide a brief review of racial identity models followed by reflection exercises to assist you in increasing awareness of your racial identity.

Cross Model

1. PRE-ENCOUNTER: individuals in the pre-encounter phase tend to range from low salience to race neutrality to anti-Black sentiments (Cross, 1991). Typically, the person seeks to assimilate to the dominant White culture and may distance themselves from Black culture, with an underlying belief that Whiteness is good and Blackness is bad. Little to

no emphasis is given to their race and they may attribute stressors to other events due to their notions that race is not a factor in their daily lives. Some may foster an anti-Black mentality. Cross (1991) stated that "anti-Blacks loath other Blacks; they feel alienated from them and do not see Blacks or the Black community as potential or actual sources of personal support" (p. 191).

Given that the individual is largely unaware of racial implications and may not understand that they have been socialized to favor Eurocentric values, you as the clinician may have to be aware of potential triggers in the session for yourself and not push your values and ideologies on the patient in a way that may feel jarring for the client. The ultimate goal is to reduce the effects of racial trauma and to hopefully engender healthy racial identity and empowerment. In cases such as these, we may have to take a more circuitous route in order to reach those objectives. You may have to gently highlight the ways in which upholding Eurocentric values are negatively impacting the patient and foster a greater understanding into how they relate to their Blackness as an individual in the larger scope of society.

2. ENCOUNTER: this stage is brought on by an event or series of events that forces the individual to acknowledge the impact of racism in their life and the reality that they can't truly be White and must focus on their identity within a marginalized group targeted by racism. It is important to note that this event may be positive or negative.

3. IMMERSION/EMERSION: according to Cross (1991) this stage represents "the most sensational aspect of Black identity development, for it represents the vortex of psychological nigrescence." It is marked by two separate but related Immersion Identities and is in contrast to the pre-encounter phase. In this phase anything African or Afrocentric is considered good (Intense Black Involvement) and anything White is considered to be evil (Anti-White Sentiments). Consequently, in this phase the person will

actively seek out opportunities to deepen their knowledge of their African identity and will seek out support from those of their own racial background. These endeavors are seen as positive, however, the person is often burdened by feelings of rage, anxiety, and guilt that are potentially destructive to their overall well-being if not properly managed. This rage and anxiety is often directed towards Whites or African Americans that they view in the pre-encounter phase or those that hold multiculturalist views. They may also feel anger and guilt towards themselves for not realizing the impact of racism sooner and taking action (Vandiver, Fhagen-Smith, Cokley, Cross, & Worrell, 2001). Anti-White attitudes are an inevitable consequence of full immersion into one's Black identity. The individual may denigrate White culture or have fantasies about obtaining retribution from the dominant culture and anti-White attitudes can become a permanent feature of the person's identity (Cross, 1991).

4. INTERNALIZATION: in this stage, the individual has a more secure racial identity. As a result, their pro-Black attitudes become less defensive and more open and expansive. They are willing to establish meaningful relationships with Whites who acknowledge and respect their Black identity. Additionally, they are ready to build alliances with members of other oppressed groups.

5. INTERNALIZATION-COMMITMENT: in this final stage, the person has discovered ways to translate their positive Black identity into a plan of action or commitment to the concerns of their racial group. This is sustained over time. The individual conveys a sense of comfort in their race and the races of those around them. Their race becomes the safe base and launching pad for them to explore new ideas, cultures, and experiences.

Conceptualizing Race-Based Stress Using the Cross Model

Carter et al. (2017) found that those in these earlier stages (Conformity, Dissonance, Immersion-Emersion) of racial identity development had higher rates of race-based traumatic stress. These findings suggest that individuals can still be psychologically harmed without a sophisticated understanding of race, which is typically seen in the Conformity and Dissonance stages. Individuals who don't view race as a factor may be more susceptible to internalizing the cause of an event to personal characteristics (Comas-Díaz, 2016). Consequently, as the therapist, it will be important for you to assess their level of awareness and facilitate the individual being able to accurately label racial incidents (Helms, 1996). Moreover, for those in the Immersion-Emersion stage, they may have more recently become aware of race. As a result, they may be hypervigilant to threats in every circumstance and not limit it to those that are similar and appropriate. The person may begin to oscillate between internalizing and externalizing their feelings onto others (Carter et al., 2017). Additionally, a lack of understanding of racial dynamics may leave them without the coping strategies necessary to effectively navigate these instances. The individual may be vulnerable to overwhelming emotional experiences in response to these traumatic events and have no direction on how to heal and move forward. Research supports that those in Internalization stages overall experience lower levels of RBS. It has been postulated that this may be due to internalized identities and more effective coping strategies leading to less psychological distress from racial events (Carter et al., 2017; Forsyth & Carter, 2012; Bryant-Davis & Ocampo, 2005).

Helms' (2008) White Racial Identity Development

1. CONTACT: this stage is characterized by a lack of awareness of White privilege and the enduring effects of racism. The person may hold a "colorblind" mentality. The person may see race, but not think it has any relevance to how they are treated in society. Additionally, they may have limited contact with people of color overall.
2. DISENTIGRATION: this stage is marked by increasing awareness of the struggles of people of color and the role that Whites play in maintaining systemic racism.

Consequently, this new information often leads to feelings of guilt, shame, and in some cases anger. If channeled through positive outlets, these feelings can subside. However, many experience societal pressure to maintain the status quo, which leads them to reintegration.

3. REINTEGRATION: due to the tremendous influence of society, the person may become more strongly aligned with their racial group. They may acknowledge the privilege of Whites, but see them as deserved. A notable characteristic of this phase is the tendency to blame the victim. Consequently, they may see people of color as the source of their problems. For instance, someone in this phase may make statements like, "if he had complied with officer, he wouldn't have been shot," even if the person was unarmed.

4. PSEUDO-INDEPENDENT: this is the first stage of positive racial identity development. Generally speaking, the person has abandoned the idea of White superiority. However, they may still unintentionally act in ways that perpetuate systems of oppression. People in this stage have the tendency to be information seeking. They are learning more about people of color and supportive of their efforts to confront racism. However, the individual doesn't yet how to maintain the balance of a positive White identity and a stance of anti-racism. As a result, missteps may occur in this phase as they are finding their path towards allyship.

5. IMMERSION/EMERSION: in this stage the person continues self-exploration. They begin to redefine their Whiteness. They seek out knowledge from other Whites who have learned how to be anti-racist allies.

6. AUTONOMY: this stage is marked by a newly defined White identity. The feelings of guilt, shame, and anger are reduced. The person has positive connections to self and has desires to participate in social justice. They are more knowledgeable about the issues of race and not fearful to approach and confront the realities of oppression in daily life.

Identifying Your Racial Identity and How It Developed

After reviewing the models above, you may have begun to think about your racial/ethnic identity and how it developed. In doing so, consider all the shaping events and people throughout your life. What stories have you heard about your race from your family of origin? What stories have you heard about other racial/ethnic groups? We are all products of our shared family stories, education, social exposure, and sociopolitical environment. It is unrealistic to believe that we do not carry some form of racism, prejudice, or biases. In fact, it can be assumed that without intentional reflection, no one is inoculated or untouched by our racial constructs. Acknowledge and accept as fact you are a product of your conditioning and have inherited the biases of society. Your ability to practice honest self-reflection on race is an act of anti-racism, leading to increased awareness around biases (both positive and negative). It is important that you get comfortable with your story.

Increased awareness of your racial identity is directly connected to your cultural competence. Reflective practices are not about identifying deficits in cultural competence, which can be threatening to any provider, but about exploring what is there non-judgmentally and making wise-minded decisions about what is helpful and harmful. Be mindful of the emphasis on practice versus obtaining competence. There is no true finish line in this reflection, but a commitment to lifelong learning. Maintain humble reflection on how one's knowledge is always partial, incomplete, and inevitably biased. Practice results in an ability to stay open and other-oriented when clients are talking about identity in ways that raise our anxiety. Therefore, practice is what facilitates your ability to assist your clients in the same process in building resilience and increasing a sense of empowerment. Worksheets 1.2 and 1.3 (The Black Awakening and Racial Perceptions) at the end of this chapter may assist your reflective practice.

Racial Identity and Professional Identity Development

In addition to developing your practice of self-reflection on your racial/ethnic identity, specific attention may need to be paid to how it is consolidated with your professional identity. Becoming a mental health professional is a considerable undertaking involving the transformation of identity at the professional level as well as personal level (Melton, Shrader, & Baca 2014). Though there has been little focus on the impact of one's cultural and ethnic identity on professional identity development, the literature acknowledges that the practice of mental health professionals reflects the society within which it is embedded and is perpetuated by its foundations (Tinsley-Jones, 2001). Consequently, the traditions of professions in mental health are not only influenced by society's contemporary biases, prejudices, and racism, but also by biases, prejudices, and racism ingrained in its historical foundation. These influences on the profession of mental health are reflected at the collegial level as well as in the services rendered to minority clients. Additional reflection questions on the consolidation of your professional and personal identities (in as much as this is possible) are identified in Box 1.1.

Box 1.1: Reflection Questions for Consolidating Professional and Racial/Ethnic Identity(ies)

What does it mean to you to be a mental health professional?

From your experience, what is the most important element in being a mental health professional?

What experiences stood out to you in becoming a mental health professional?

How would you describe your racial/ethnic identity?

What does it mean to you to identify as _____?

How has race/ethnicity come up in your professional life?

Were there any specific training experiences that influenced the integration of your professional and racial/ethnic identity? If so, in what ways?

Were there any situations from your field experiences that influenced the integration of your professional and racial/ethnic identity? If so, in what ways?

Were there significant relationships that influenced the integration of your professional and racial/ethnic identity? If so, in what ways?

WORKSHEET 1.1: ADDRESSING MODEL

Cultural Influence	Dominant Group	Non-Dominant Group
Age and generational influences		
Developmental or other **D**isability		
Religious and spiritual orientation		
Ethnic and racial identity		
Socioeconomic status		
Sexual orientation		
Indigenous heritage		
National origin		
Gender		

Copyright material from Monica M. Johnson and Michelle L. Melton (2021), *Addressing Race-Based Stress in Therapy with Black Clients*, Taylor & Francis

WORKSHEET 1.2: THE BLACK AWAKENING

Think back to your earliest memories and try to recall when you first recognized the individual and social impact of being a Black person in the world. Describe the event in as much detail as possible and use additional sheets of paper if necessary. Make sure to address the following questions, but do not limit yourself to these questions. This is just meant as a guide to help the process. How old were you? What happened? Were you alone? If you were with others, what were their responses and how did that influence you? What thoughts do you recall? What feelings do you recall? What messages did you receive about your race from this experience? Do you consider this experience to be positive or negative and why?

Copyright material from Monica M. Johnson and Michelle L. Melton (2021), *Addressing Race-Based Stress in Therapy with Black Clients*, Taylor & Francis

WORKSHEET 1.3: RACIAL PERCEPTIONS

We obtain messages about our race from multiple sources including our family and friends, the media, and the larger society, etc. In these various areas write down the messages you've received, where it came from, place a + if you consider it to be positive and – if you consider it to be a negative message, and ± if neutral. In the final area, rate how much you believe in this message from 0–5 (0 being not true at all and 5 very true). Return this handout to your therapist to further explore racial perceptions and their impact.

1. Physical Appearance and Attributes: body type/shape, perceived attributes, facial features, skin tone, hair, style of dress, etc.

Message	Origin	Perception	Belief

Copyright material from Monica M. Johnson and Michelle L. Melton (2021), *Addressing Race-Based Stress in Therapy with Black Clients*, Taylor & Francis

2. Personality: the personality characteristics are assumed of Black people

Message	Origin	Perception	Belief

3. Mental Functioning: intelligence, school performance, ability to reason or problem solve, judgment

Message	Origin	Perception	Belief

4. Sexuality: sex, sexual attractiveness, sexuality

Message	Origin	Perception	Belief

How do you feel about the messages you've received?

What affect do these messages have on your daily living if any?

CHAPTER 2

Re-envisioning Ethics Through a Multicultural-Oriented Framework

Introduction

As professionals, we work to promote mental health and treat mental disorders. Our work is shaped by ethical principles and professional codes of conduct, guiding the use of our science and expertise to benefit society. The cultural competence movement in mental health also emphasizes the appropriate provision of services to the benefit of all people. It establishes the importance of culture in people's lives, respect for cultural differences, and minimization of any negative consequences of cultural differences in the provision of mental health care. In this sense, cultural competence and professional ethics are mutually supportive practices for the respect for persons, beneficence, nonmaleficence, and justice (Hoop, DiPasquale, Hernandez, & Roberts, 2008). In this chapter we further delineate multicultural competence as an ethical imperative and will present culturally informed ethical decision-making models for practical use.

From Personal to Professional: Nuancing Multiculturalism and Ethics

Ethical principles are an expression of moral ideals and values, which are a product of human culture (Hoop et al., 2008;

Rogers-Sirin & Sirin, 2009). Because values are culturally mediated, your deliberations when faced with ethically challenging clinical situations are to some degree a product of your own personal cultural development and heritage. Your awareness of your cultural identity(ies) and morals, then, play an important role in shaping your ethical professional practice. By acknowledging that your personal morals and values influence adherence to professional ethical standards, you also challenge and refute paradigms that emphasize neutrality (Bhola & Chaturvedi, 2017). For example, when a practitioner's values reflect the dominant discourse on patriarchy, there may be less sensitivity to the autonomy and rights of female patients, potentially leading to violations of justice as an ethical principle. Additionally, a professional's personal cultural development and heritage may evoke strong negative feelings when faced with clients' behaviors or disclosures that reflect values not shared by the professional (Bhola & Chaturvedi, 2017; Hoop et al., 2008). Consider for example, a monogamous therapist's reaction to a client seeking help in managing stress related to polyamorous relationships with four other people. If the therapist holds unconscious bias toward monogamous relationships, she or he may attempt to help the client reduce stress by creating a plan to leave the polyamorous relationship. In this way, the therapist may be unaware of imposing his or her values on the health and healing of the client.

The differences in personal values between you and your client(s) is a significant consideration in treatment as research has demonstrated our values influence the effectiveness of therapy. As discussed in Chapter 1, you are co-creating cultural expression with your clients. As your values differ from those of your clients, the power differential inherent in the role of therapist will influence and change your clients' values (Kocet & Herlihy, 2014). Awareness of your cultural values, power position, and clients' values will help mitigate undue influence. Therefore, it is imperative that you address and integrate a multicultural framework as a practical, concrete demonstration of your professional ethical principles.

The integration of culture and ethics is exhibited by learning about culture, embracing pluralism, and proactive accommodation

(Paasche-Orlow, 2004). By adopting a multicultural orientation, the practitioner embraces a dialectic of moral pluralism and ethical relativism (Beauchamp, 2014). A dialectical stance allows for the synthesizing of viewpoints. In other words, as a multiculturally competent practitioner, you can maintain an open-minded stance when confronted with competing or conflicting moral viewpoints while holding that each are worthy of respect. This open-minded stance is grounded in the belief that nothing is objectively right or wrong and that the definition of right or wrong depends on the prevailing moral norms of the individual, culture, or historical period (Beauchamp, 2014). Therefore, the issue is not maintaining "professional objectivity," but the application of a multicultural framework. Consequently, ethical codes and practices can be more inclusive and contextualized in ethical deliberation of best care practices (Durante, 2017).

In addition to your personal cultural heritage, you also negotiate the knowledge, beliefs, laws, morals, and the customs of health care culture. The health care culture shapes the ethics and values of professionals in ways that may be foreign or culturally incongruent to the individuals and community served. The term health care refers to the organizational structure consisting of interrelated components including institutions, resources, people, market participants, government regulations, and funding. Policy in many health care systems delineates the scope of ethics and articulates the values and culture of the system and institution (Greppert & Shelton, 2016). In the United States, it can be argued that the health care system is based on Western European concepts of health, healing, and capitalism. Consequently, health care disparities may be a biproduct of the cultural incongruencies between US health care culture and its diverse communities (Thomas, Fine, & Ibrahim, 2004). Over the past decade, movements to address social, cultural, and environmental factors beyond the biomedical model of health care have exhibited sustained urgency to eliminate health care disparities. Inherent in this commitment to reduce inequalities is a shift in health care culture to be more responsive to and actively engage participation of affected individuals and communities in the creation of health communication interventions and the consideration of culture in message development (Thomas et al., 2004). As an ethical, multiculturally competent professional, you may take a leading role in shifting health care systems from a paternalistic, practitioner-driven culture toward a more client-centered, multiculturally oriented culture.

Integrating Multiculturalism and Ethical Practice

Ethical codes of conduct set forth by mental health professional organizations emphasize professional standards, objectivity, and neutrality, as well as outline the values of the profession. For example, the American Psychological Association's Ethical Principles and Code of Conduct for Psychologists (2017) outline the highest ideals of psychology, emphasizing professional beneficence (doing good), nonmaleficence (not doing harm), and justice (treating people fairly). Additionally, the American Counseling Association's Code of Ethics (2014), American Psychiatric Association's Principles of Medical Ethics (2013b), American Psychiatric Nurses Association Code of Ethics for Nurses (2015), and National Association of Social Workers (2017) also set the "essentials of honorable behavior" to include:

- Autonomy, fidelity, compassion, and respect for human dignity and rights
- Honesty in all professional actions
- Responsible participation in improving community and public health
- Support of access to care for all people

These cornerstones of ethical codes reflect the aspirational values of the profession and the work. The application of ethics codes includes the "habitual and judicious use of communication, knowledge, technical skills, clinical reasoning, emotions, values, and reflection in daily practice for the benefit of the individual and community being served" (Epstein & Hundert, 2002, p. 226). It is a consistent practice versus holding a *belief* about the importance of ethics in practice. The practice involves ethical sensitivity, ethical judgment, and ethical choice applied in a sequence of logical steps (Louw, 2016). In other words, you will do well to have a model for ethical decisions and practices that is informed by multicultural theory and literature.

Ethico-cultural Decision-Making Model for Mental Health Practice

Integrating a multicultural orientation into an ethical framework will support you as a sociocultural being, living and practicing in a political society, with common public ethics to guide ethical practices. Having an articulated model will protect your clients, promote quality care, and support your development and reflective practice. You will also be better able to incorporate social justice in practice by considering individuals' and communities' contextual elements (e.g., historical marginalized, oppression, etc). Developing an ethico-cultural decision model will involve considerations of your personal and professional identities, treatment context, and treatment models. To align with a moral pluralist understanding of multiculturalism, a social constructivist foundation for developing an ethico-cultural model is recommended. A social constructivist approach acknowledges that decisions are not made solely in the head of the therapist but are co-created with the client and/or other stakeholders (i.e. families, communities, agencies, regulatory bodies, etc.). Additionally, the therapist considers the social context of the client community (i.e. urban/suburban/rural setting, high or low income/resource market, etc.) and the impact any decision made will have on the client and her or his community. This approach also provides an avenue for negotiating competing needs between the therapist, client, and agency/institution to increase consensual agreement for engaging in services and settling disputes when necessary (Cottone, 2004). The Transcultural Integrative Ethical Decision-Making Model is our recommended model that integrates social constructivist concepts and multicultural theory. Following a step-by-step, linear process, this model is an inclusive ethico-cultural approach for reflective, balanced ethical-decision making process for you, your client(s), and other stakeholders (Garcia, Cartwright, Winston, & Borzuchowska, 2003). Providing an extensive review of this model is beyond the scope of this text. However, the relevant steps of the model are below.

Step 1: Interpreting the Situation Through Awareness and Fact Finding. The goals of this step are to (1) increase awareness about the potential dilemma, (2) determine if it is an actual dilemma, identify the stakeholders involved, and (3) engage in a process of fact finding. Subcategories include:

- Enhancement of sensitivity and awareness
- Reflection to analyze whether a dilemma is involved
- Determination of major stakeholders
- Engagement in the fact-finding process

Step 2: Formulating an Ethical Decision. You will examine ethical codes of your profession, rules, and statues in law to determine if they contain applicable diversity standards. This examination will help to identify potentially discriminatory laws, institutional policies/procedures from a cultural perspective. Subcategories of this step include:

- Review the dilemma
- Determine ethical codes, laws, ethical principles, institution policies, and procedures
- Generate courses of action and consider potential positive and negative consequences for each course of action
- Consultation
- Select the best ethical course of action

Step 3: Weighing Competing Nonmoral Values and Affirming the Course of Action. Lack of consideration of personal biases and self–interest may increase the possibility of engaging in unethical behaviors. This step includes the following:

- Engage in reflective recognition and analysis of personal blind spots
- Consider contextual influences on values selection

Step 4: Planning and Executing the Selected Course of Action. Lastly, you will carry out the plan, document the process, and evaluate the consequences. Substeps include:

- Develop a reasonable sequence of concrete actions
- Anticipate personal and contextual barriers and counter measures
- Implementation, documentation, and evaluation of the course of action

Applying the Transcultural Integrative Ethical Decision-Making Model: Case Scenario

Dr. Woods (Persian-American, male) is a psychologist at a large urban private health care system. He recently received a referral to evaluate a 20-year-old Afro-Latina woman. The referral came from a physician (White, male) in the primary care clinic at the agency. The referring physician stated:

> Patient is actively engaged in prostitution and is requesting the medication prEP to prevent contracting HIV. A mental health examination is warranted as the patient plans to continue to prostitute. She is likely experiencing behavioral health issues that result in this continued risky behavior.

The physician did not administer any behavioral health screeners or indicate if mental health symptoms were endorsed by the patient. The referring physician has submitted the referral without informing the patient. Dr. Woods is unsure if accepting the referral will reinforce the patient's risky behavior or if declining the referral will prevent the patient from receiving the requested care.

The case of Dr. Woods raises several ethical concerns that are unique and challenging. The Transcultural Integrative Ethical Decision-Making Model is useful in confronting the ethical dilemma(s) Dr. Woods may be facing. Additionally, we reference the American Psychological Association's Ethical Principles of Psychologists and Code of Conduct (2017) to assist in identifying the best course of action to address the referral.

Step 1: Interpreting the Situation through Awareness and Fact Finding

Enhancement of Sensitivity and Awareness

Dr. Woods considers the needs and welfare of parties involved in the dilemma including himself, the patient, and the referring physician. The patient's needs have been clearly identified in the referral (e.g., prescribed PrEP to prevent contracting HIV). Even though Dr. Woods has not yet met the patient, it is important for him to be aware of his attitude and biases regarding sex workers as well as his cultural competence with sex worker culture. He is conscious of the power differential that may have existed between the White, male physician, and the Afro-Latina, female patient. Dr. Woods is also sensitive to politics of gender, and differences in socially condoned behaviors between genders.

Reflection to Analyze Whether a Dilemma Is Involved

In this scenario, Dr. Woods' initial reservation involved whether completing the evaluation would reinforce the patient's "risky behavior" or if the patient's request would be denied if the evaluation was not completed. Dr. Woods now recognizes the former thought was influenced more by his own biases about sex workers than clinical considerations. The latter thought appears to reflect considerations about the patient's welfare in addition to cooperation with other professionals and adhering to organizational practices. He becomes aware that the basis of the referral may not be sound given that (1) no informed consent for the referral was obtained and (2) no objective or subjective data were included in the referral indicating the presence of behavioral health needs. Dr. Woods now wonders if completing the evaluation would be considered "fraud, waste, or abuse" of services and billing.

Determination of Major Stakeholders

The stakeholders in this scenario are Dr. Woods, the patient, and the physician. Another potential stakeholder with ethical and legal relationship to the patient is the health care system. Stakeholders may also be expanded to include any other patients that the referring physician or Dr. Woods may see for primary care or psychological services. For example, patient experience (i.e. the product of an interaction between an organization and a patient over the duration of their relationship) in receiving care may be negatively impacted by perceived discrimination and/or denial of services. The reputation of the services rendered by the health care system will thus be tainted. Subsequently, community members' help seeking behaviors may decrease, thereby increasing health care disparities and decreasing population health in underserved communities.

Engagement in the Fact-finding Process

Dr. Woods thoroughly reviews the patient's electronic health record (EHR) for any missed information regarding the referral. He begins to research information about sex worker culture and rights. Additionally, Dr. Woods considers the dynamics and influences of the genders, ethnicities, and socioeconomic statuses of the stakeholders (e.g. referring physician, patient, and Dr. Woods). He reviews agency policy regarding consultations and referrals for services between clinics. Next, Dr. Woods consults the relevant codes of ethics in addition to the state psychology board's statues and rules regarding the conduct of psychologists. Lastly, he reviews the psychological literature regarding managing values conflicts with patients.

Step 2: Formulating an Ethical Decision

Review the Dilemma

After collecting further information and carefully considering all the cultural factors involved in the dilemma, Dr. Woods determines there are potential violations of several American Psychological Association ethical principles and codes of conduct. Additionally, there are potential violations of organizational policy and practice as outline by the health care system's standard operative procedures (SOP).

Determine Ethical Codes, Laws, Ethical Principles, Institution Policies, and Procedures

For the purpose of this scenario the following APA codes were reviewed and applied:

2.04 Bases for Scientific and Professional Judgments

3.07 Third-Party Requests for Services

3.09 Cooperation with Other Professionals

3.10 Informed Consent

3.11 Psychological Services Delivered to or Through Organizations

9.01 Bases for Assessments

9.03 Informed Consent in Assessments

Generate Courses of Action and Consider Potential Positive and Negative Consequences for Each Course of Action

There are four potential courses of actions for Dr. Woods to consider. To assist in exploring each course of action, we created a table to analyze each option using APA ethic principles.

1. Dr. Woods will contact the patient to schedule to complete the requested evaluation.

Ethical Principle	Compliant	Violated	Justification
Beneficence and Nonmaleficence		x	Informed consent has not been obtained from the patient for an evaluation. Calling to schedule for unrequested services, with no clinical basis, overpathologizes the patient and is a discriminative practice.
Fidelity and Responsibility		x	Informed consent has not been established.

Integrity	x	There is no scientific evidence or evidence-based practice establishing psychological testing for prEP as clinically warranted.
Justice	x	Patient is being treated differently due to engaging in sex work.
Respect for People's Rights and Dignity	x	Patient is asking for medication to manage her health. There has been no endorsement of mental health or behavioral health concerns by the patient.

2. Dr. Woods declines the referral for evaluation.

Ethical Principle	Compliant	Violated	Justification
Beneficence and Nonmaleficence	x		Informed consent has not been obtained from the patient for an evaluation. It is not clear that psychology services will directly impact this case.
Fidelity and Responsibility		x	Dr. Woods did not consult with the referring physician to the extent needed to serve the patient. He also did not address any concerns about the physician's ethical compliance or professional conduct regarding this referral.

(continued)

Ethical Principle	Compliant	Violated	Justification
Integrity	x		Dr. Woods did not engage in an unwise or unclear commitment.
Justice	x		Dr. Woods did not condone an unjust practice of referring patients for services without consent or singling out specific patients for services that are not clinically indicated.
Respect for People's Rights and Dignity	x		Dr. Woods maintains the patient's right to privacy, confidentiality, and self-determination.

3. Dr. Woods contacts the referring physician to clarify the rationale for the referral.

Ethical Principle	Compliant	Violated	Justification
Beneficence and Nonmaleficence	x		Dr. Woods can seek clarity in case the physician did not document all relevant information in the referral. Discussing the referral directly with the physician may also allow Dr. Woods to share any concerns of value-based judgments being made that may influence treatment decisions. He can also provide education regarding the informed
Fidelity and Responsibility	x		
Integrity	x		
Justice	x		
Respect for People's Rights and Dignity	x		

consent process and parameters for psychological assessment. Dr. Woods and the physician are be able to collaborate on the best care possible to meet the patient's needs.

4. Dr. Woods contacts the patient to clarify mental health needs.

Ethical Principle	Compliant	Violated	Justification
Beneficence and Nonmaleficence		x	Informed consent has not been obtained for the assessment. Calling the patient and explaining the referral could validate the concept that patient needs a mental health evaluation based solely on being a sex worker.
Fidelity and Responsibility		x	Informed consent violation.
Integrity		x	Not in line with best practice standards for psychological assessment.
Justice		x	Patient is being treated differently due to engaging in sex work.
Respect for People's Rights and Dignity		x	Patient is asking for medication to manage her health. There has been no endorsement of mental health or behavioral health concerns by the patient.

Consultation

It may be helpful to approach the health care system's ethics committee or the legal representatives at the executive level for consultation. Consultation with experts can provide insights and the most recent scientific, legal, and ethical developments with a culturally sensitive lens.

Select the Best Ethical Course of Action

The best course of action would be to have a conversation with the referring physician to clarify the referral and/or inform him of the reasons the referral will be declined. At the same time, the physician would be strongly encouraged to reflect on his reasons for making the referral and to consult his profession's ethical guidelines to better inform his practice. If the physician is unable to discuss the case, the next best option is to decline the referral. Dr. Woods can document his reasoning and rationale for declining the referral should questions arise.

Step 3: Weighing Competing Nonmoral Values and Affirming the Course of Action

Engage in Reflective Recognition and Analysis of Personal Blind Spots

Consideration of personal biases, self-interest, nonmoral values, and systematic biases and interests can reduce likelihood of engaging in unethical behaviors. For example, Dr. Woods reflects on personal biases (i.e. positive biases for the rights of sex workers, negative biases toward medical doctors, etc.), self-interests (i.e. not wanting to add another evaluation to his current workload), nonmoral values (i.e. wanting to be a well liked and respected provider at the agency), and systematic biases (i.e. decreasing need to add expensive, new medications to the facility formulary).

Consider Contextual Influences on Values Selection

A significant contextual influence is current societal attitudes and legal/law enforcement perspectives on sex work and sex workers. Moral judgments about sex work have expanded across centuries, countries, and cultures. Contemporary debates center on two views that sex work is: (1) the cause or consequence of trafficking, exploitation, and violence; (2) consensual sex between adults for monetary gain (Tandon, Armas-Cardona, & Grover, 2014). It has also been documented that sex workers routinely face physical and sexual violence, arrest and incarceration, extortion and harassment, forced medical interventions, and denial of health care, housing, and legal protections (Murphy, 2015). Consideration of these factors may influence values selection (e.g., health care clinics denying services or forcing unwanted medical/behavioral health procedures as a deterrent to engage in sex work).

Step 4: Planning and Executing the Selected Course of Action

Develop a Reasonable Sequence of Concrete Actions

The chosen course of action is to discuss the referral directly with the physician. The goals of the discussion are to clarify if the patient endorsed behavioral health symptoms and consented to engage in the evaluation. Dr. Woods can also clarify if the physician has prescribed prEP or if the prescription is contingent upon the completion of the psychological evaluation. Given the responses to Dr. Woods' questions, he and the physician can develop a plan to address the needs of the patient.

Anticipate Personal and Contextual Barriers and Counter Measures

It can be anticipated that disagreement about the merits of the referral may arise. In this case, Dr. Woods can engage in more focused dialog to illuminate if cultural barriers (i.e. biases, discriminations, stereotypes, prejudices) might be influencing the disagreement. Dr. Woods can share information and new knowledge he has gathered as well as highlight professional ethics codes and/or agency policies to resolve the dilemma. Dr. Woods would also do well to take a relational approach to addressing the dilemma with the physician. His duty is not to judge or punish, but instead, if needed, leave such steps to the administrative or legal authorities.

Implementation, Documentation, and Evaluation of the Course of Action

Dr. Woods should document all deliberations completed on his own as well as consultation sought. Thorough documentation of the discussion and outcome with the physician is also warranted.

The Transcultural Integrative Model is a useful tool to address ethical dilemmas while honoring the cultural factors that may play an important if not definitive role. We hope this model will serve as a valuable reference for ethical dilemmas.

Managing Value Conflicts

Basing culturally competent care on ethical principles provides a foundation in the provision of services as well as addressing dilemmas related to different cultural values. As previously mentioned, a professional's cultural heritage and moral values are inherent in the services provided. At times, conflicts may arise between your values and those of your client. It is not expected that you abandon your values to align with those of your client. It is also not expected that you refer out when value conflicts do arise. At worst, referring out based on the belief that your client's presenting concern is in conflict with your sincerely held values may be an act of discrimination and/or a microaggression. This is especially true if you make such a decision without first (1) engaging in discussion with your client, or (2) seeking supervision, consultation, or continuing education to increase your capacity to provide services. In this case, the referral could be considered inappropriate and a violation of ethical practice (Shiles, 2009). Ford and Hendrick (2003) found that when confronted with a values conflict with a client, only 18% of professionals consulted with a colleague, 4% engaged in self-examination, sought additional information, or viewed the issue from the client perspective, and 1% helped the client explored the issue. These findings suggest that many professionals may be engaging in discriminatory referrals and, potentially, unethical practices. The literature offers contradictory advice on managing value conflicts, at times arguing against values-based referrals as well as acknowledging that such referrals are appropriate in rare instances (Kocet & Herlihy, 2014). Therefore, having a sound approach, grounded in a multicultural framework, for reasoning through value conflicts will aid you in delivering the best standard of care. Kocet and Herlihy (2014) provide a practical, value-driven, multiculturally oriented, ethical, decision-making process to address values conflicts that may be used to guide professional practice.

Step One: Identification of the Concern, the Values Conflict

The first step in a decision-making process is to explicitly identify the ethical concern or question. A clear statement allows for reflection on the scope, perspective, or assumptions inherent in the dilemma, while decreasing likelihood of misleading or ambiguous concerns. Consequently, you may be better able to identify the values conflict and the nature of the conflict being either personal or professional, or both. Personal value conflicts can stem from your cultural heritage, morals, beliefs, etc. Professional conflicts can also involve both "health care culture" practices and policies, as well as professional competency issues (i.e. lacking requisite skills or training). Returning to Dr. Woods' scenario, this first step is exemplified in his determining whether the referral had a clinical basis or may be influenced by his own or the physician's personal values.

Step Two: Explore Core Issues and Potential Barriers

After clarifying the value conflict, examine what is at the core of the value conflict. As previously mentioned, conflicts can stem from your personal and/or professional values. It may be helpful to apply a two-prong approach to thoroughly evaluate both (Kocet & Herlihy, 2014). In other words, first engage in self-reflection or seek supervision regarding your personal beliefs/values at play. The goal of this reflection is not to determine whether your values, or your client's, are right or wrong, but to identify where the core conflict may lie. Next, consider previous training/work experiences with with the client population (i.e. LGBTQ+, child/

adolescent, immigrant, etc.) and treatment modality (i.e. play therapy, Christian counseling, emotional freedom technique, etc.). What continuing education activities, supervision, consultation might you have engaged in to address the client's concern? After reflecting on both your personal values and professional expertise/experience, you will be better able to articulate the core issue and barriers at play in the conflict. In the case of Dr. Woods, his reflection yielded increased awareness of both professional (i.e. no informed consent was obtained for the referral, lack of training and experience providing services to someone in the sex worker culture) and personal (i.e. belief that women should have the right to choose what happens to their bodies, negative biases against medical doctors) values conflict.

Step Three: Seek Consultation

Once the value conflict and the nature of the conflict have been explored, practitioners can seek assistance to address the conflict to provide the appropriate level of care. Reviewing ethical standards and/or the professional literature, provides guidance on both personal and professional value conflicts. Principle D of the ethics code for psychologists states,

> Psychologists recognize that fairness and justice entitle all persons to access to and benefit from the contributions of psychology ... [and] exercise reasonable judgment and take precautions to ensure that their potential biases, the boundaries of their competence, and the limitations of their expertise do not lead to or condone unjust practices.
>
> (American Psychological Association, 2017, p. 4)

Principal C for the same code instructs practitioners be "aware of their professional and scientific responsibilities to society and to the specific communities in which they work" (American Psychological Association, 2017, p. 3). These ethical principles and professional values assert that you have the responsibility to have awareness of and eliminate bias. In doing so, you are better able to provide fair and just services. As previously stated, your awareness of and elimination of biases, coupled with knowledge of the social structures affecting the communities in which services are provided, increases competence and the provision of culturally relevant care.

In addition to reviewing the standards of practice, consulting with colleagues or supervisors provides additional guidance. Consultation with other competent professionals may help you develop a remediation plan to increase technical skills, knowledge, and expertise. Seeking additional supervision or training may also address the professional competency needs. When addressing personal values conflict, consultation with others may allow you to identify ways in which personal biases/judgments are influencing professional work. Consultation can also assist with identifying ways to maintain personal values, morals, religious beliefs while providing effective services to the client. In the above scenario with Dr. Woods, he consulted the agency's ethics committee to address the professional issue. He should also be intentional in addressing personal values or biases by consulting with or receiving supervision from trusted colleagues.

Applying ethical bracketing (EB) may prove to be particularly helpful in maintaining a multicultural orientation while avoiding the imposition of your values on the client. EB is the practice of intentional separation of personal values from professional values (Kocet & Herlihy, 2014). The goal of ethical bracketing is to provide ethical and appropriate services to all clients, especially those whose world views, values, belief systems, and decisions differ from yours. The practice of bracketing is consistent with the intrapersonal and interpersonal aspects of cultural humility. More specifically, EB is the application of having an accurate perception of your own cultural values as well as maintaining an other-oriented perception that involves respect, lack of superiority, and attunement regarding your own cultural beliefs and values. Ethical bracketing skill is developed and maintained through self-reflective practices and consultation with trusted others.

Step Four: Determine and Evaluate Possible Courses of Action

If the values conflict is not resolved following the application of the first three steps, you may identify and evaluate an alternative course of action. The plan of action should reflect the examination of the nature of the values conflict and identify appropriate activities for remediation, i.e. continuing education training, additional supervision, or referral to another practitioner. It is imperative you ensure that the proposed actions promote client welfare.

Summary

Multicultural competence is imperative for ethical provision of services. The multicultural and transactional nature of cultural contexts influences the perceptions, interpretations, and the negotiation of ethical practice. Addressing cultural competence emphasizes the professional, ethical requirement to recognize and take action against discrimination and intolerance. In this way, the adoption of culturally competent skills is not a personal decision based on internal values but is rather a call to the profession. Adopting an ethico-cultural framework for practice not only protects your clients and promotes good care, but it can also negate any incongruencies between professional ethical paradigms and multicultural practices. The culturally competent clinician who promotes ethical principles will be better able to provide evidence-based therapy while addressing race-based stress injuries.

CHAPTER 3
Advocacy and Consultation Regarding Race-Based Stress

Introduction

The role of an advocate is embedded in the functioning and activities of mental health professionals. In fact, codes of conduct across mental health professions call for clinicians to assist clients and client groups through empowerment, advocacy, and social action. Advocacy, then, is a specific skill set the clinician employs within the immediate treatment context as well as in the public, sociopolitical context. This chapter will (1) identify barriers to mental health care for members of the Black community, and (2) present models and methods of advocacy and consultation to address identified barriers.

Adopt a Model of Change

At the heart of advocacy and consultation is change. In each role, you should have a strategy or framework that guides the needed or suggested change. Having a framework will assist in tailoring interventions to address the identified barriers. There are many models of creating change in existence. To address systems-related issues and culture-specific barriers, we will present and integrate the ADKAR model (Hiatt, 2006) and the Transconceptual Model of Resilience and Empowerment (Brodsky & Cattaneo, 2013).

The ADKAR Model of Change

The ADKAR Model identifies the basic critical elements of the change process. It is a multipurpose, multifaceted tool that allows the advocate clinician or consultant to better frame the identified problem and make more feasible the steps to the desired outcome (Hiatt, 2006). It is goal oriented and results driven. The key elements are Awareness, Desire, Knowledge, Ability, and Reinforcement. The process of change is embedded in these critical elements. For example, awareness of the need for change and a desire to participate in and support the change is needed to move an organization or community from its current state. Awareness and desire, once cultivated, are not enough to make a successful transition to the future state. Knowledge of how to change and the ability to engage in the required behaviors are crucial in implementing change. Once an organization, community, and or client has engaged in the transition, reinforcement can maintain the future desired state.

The Transconceptual Model of Empowerment and Resilience (TMER)

Brodsky and Cattaneo (2013) present the concepts of empowerment and resilience as an iterative process that starts with an individual and/or community recognizing an unsatisfying state and developing an intention or goal to change this state. Similar to the ADKAR model, once the problem state is recognized, agents of change then focus on goals utilizing resilience and empowerment processes. This model shows that resilience and empowerment are distinct concepts with separate foci of goal, action, and outcome. Resilience and empowerment processes are simultaneously linked by reflection about one's context, possibilities within that context, and the reconsidering of change goals. Goals focused on change at the individual or local level are aimed at intrapersonal actions and outcomes, including adapting (i.e. changing beliefs and/or behaviors to better respond to and engage in the social environment) and withstanding or resisting (i.e. maintaining beliefs and behaviors while holding separate incongruent social practices and ideologies) the current situation. Advocacy efforts that are conceptualized around resilience focus on change that is under the immediate control of the effected group. Empowerment activities, on the other hand, are typically focused on exo-system elements (i.e. change not under the immediate control of the actors) and are enacted socially. Such activities are aimed at changing relationships, situations, power dynamics, or contexts.

Model for Change through Resilience and Empowerment

Integrating the ADKDAR and TMER models acknowledges the interconnectivity of intrapersonal, interpersonal, and exo-systems factors (i.e. school, workplace, family social networks and neighborhood community contexts, local politics and industry) involved in creating change. For the mental health advocate or consultant, understanding and applying these processes leverages the strengths of individuals, communities, and systems to create a plan for change. We present the Model for Change Through Resilience and Empowerment (MCRE) for this purposes (see Figure 3.1 and Table 3.1).

The purpose of MCRE is to assist in managing the complexities inherent in change by being more sensitive to and effectively using the critical dimensions of resilience and empowerment. When using resilience and empowerment processing to create a change, we emphasize the advocate be aware of the context of change (i.e. magnitude of the change needed), fundamental risk (i.e. an elevated chance that aspirations and desires might not be obtainable, and heightened probability that basic needs, rights, and access to resources will be obstructed), and resources needed for change (i.e. knowledge, skills, support, etc.) (Brodsky & Cattaneo, 2013). Considerations of these dimensions of change will allow you to engage the most useful process. For example, a mental health provider working in a community mental health center has learned of a new law enforcement initiative to reduce gun violence in the community by expanding police officers' ability to stop and

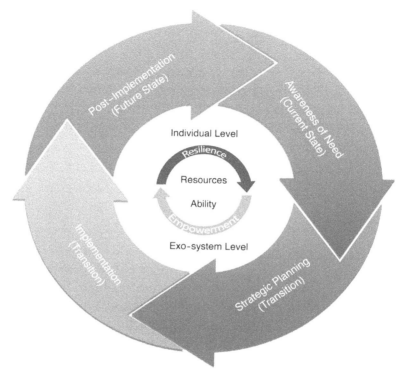

Figure 3.1 Model of Change Through Resilience and Empowerment

question "suspicious" persons. Since the initiative has been implemented, the mental health provider has had a significant decrease in her therapy show rate, which her clients attribute to increased fear of being harassed by police when out of the home. In this example, the mental health provider recognizes the disempowerment of community members (i.e. the increased authority for police to profile community members) and the effect this has had on accessing mental health care. The needed change may be to empower community members, specifically in addressing the new policing practices. The mental health provider can set a goal and intention to assist her clients in advocating for themselves by petitioning city council to end the new initiative that is creating a barrier to care. To increase client's knowledge and ability to advocate, the mental health

Table 3.1 Model of Change Through Resilience and Empowerment

Awareness of Need for Change

Resilience: emotional, cognitive sensitivity, and awareness of needs focused on the individual and microsystem (i.e. family, school, peers, church, work, neighborhood) level. Includes reflection on intrapsychic and interpersonal dimension of needs.

Empowerment: emotional, cognitive sensitivity, and awareness of needs focused on the mesosystem (i.e. extended family, friends of family, mass media, legal, health, and social services) and exo-system (i.e. economic system, political system, education system, government system, and religious system). Includes identification of the major stakeholders that have a relationship to the individual and community.

Strategic Planning

Resilience: considering available resources (self-efficacy, knowledge, coping resources, etc.), determine possible courses of action and their consequences (positive and negative). Options at this level will often fall in one of the following categories: adapt, withstand, resist. Reflection on the individual's desire for change and ability is critical. Select a course of action and identify sequential steps. Anticipate personal barriers to successful implementation. Develop effective and relevant counter measures.

Empowerment: considering available resources (resilience resources, knowledge of systems, relationship/access to stakeholders, etc.), determine possible courses of action and their consequences. Understanding of context and power dynamics is critical during the planning stage. Develop desire for change and ability to building alliances and coalitions needed. Select a course of action and identify sequential steps. Anticipate personal and contextual barriers to successful implementation. Develop effective and relevant counter measures.

Implementation

Resilience: execute course of action as planned.

Empowerment: execute course of action as planned.

Post-Implementation

Resilience and Empowerment: gather and document valid and reliable information on the accuracy of the action taken. Reflection on the process will allow for continued learning. Reinforce changes made to maintain future state.

provider can schedule groups to increase assertiveness skills. To reinforce clients' actions, the provider can offer monthly potlucks or parties to celebrate the progress made each month.

The goal and the plan outlined above follows the MCRE and may result in goal achievement to empower clients and community members. However, after identifying a needed change it is essential that the advocate or consultant also consider the contextual dimensions of fundamental risk and the magnitude of change from the current state to the desired state. The empowerment process must anticipate the fundamental risk to people in communities who lack power in the larger system. When there is a significant gap between the current state (e.g., clients afraid to leave home due to anticipated harassment from police) and desired state (e.g. ending "stop and frisk" practices by law enforcement), which is accompanied by lethal peril (i.e. among members of the Black community where speaking and acting on behalf of basic rights to law enforcement have led to arrests, bodily harm, and deaths), a feeling of empowerment and motivation to act can not only be unrealistic, but deadly. If the fundamental risk is high, the assets (i.e. resources, skills, etc.) for change are low, and there is a significant fundamental threat, the first step should be to focus on a resilience goal at the individual level.

Returning to the example, this well-meaning clinician could first develop a resilience-oriented skills group for affected clients. The goal of the group could be to increase client internal characteristics (i.e. hope, self-efficacy, motivation) as well as enhance individual assets (i.e. knowledge of systems, resources, communication skills, social support, and access to community resources). The provider can incorporate activities of resilience (described further in Chapter 6) in the group, including:

- Teaching internal coping skills to manage emotional distress related to interactions with police;
- Building assertiveness skills and bystander interventions in order effectively advocate for themselves in challenging situations;

- Identifying and growing self-worth and self-esteem;
- Helping identify resources to stay inspired and hopeful;
- Assisting to brainstorm ways to get involved in positive social change and help others;
- Increase client's knowledge of applicable laws and citizen rights, the power structure of police departments, community recourses for supporting action, etc.

Additionally, the group participants will also need to develop the ability to reflect on their actions and their impact to create the desired change. The skill of self-reflection will then allow clients to reassess and adjust actions taken to change power dynamics and relationships between clients and law enforcement. If the circumstances are favorable, the next step may be to set a new empowerment goal that moves beyond change on an individual level and aims for external change that involves an increase in power within the larger environment.

Strategic Planning for Advocacy and Consultation

Activities of advocacy or consultation should be thoughtful, strategic, and informed by a model(s) of change as previously discussed. The focus of change interventions and strategies can be individual clients, communities, organizations and systems, the public domain, and/or sociopolitical arenas. The following are suggested steps to develop a plan of advocacy, both in direct intervention as well as in a consultative role:

1. Identify barriers to the well-being of individuals and vulnerable groups;
2. Identify appropriate interventions and strategies;
3. Identify supports and potential allies and barriers;
4. Develop and implement a strategic plan;
5. Assess impact and/or effectiveness of implementation.

To illustrate the application of a plan, let us consider mental health disparities in the Black community.

Framing the Problem of Mental Health Disparities and the Black Community

The 2001 US Surgeon General Report, *Mental Health: Culture, Race, and Ethnicity*, documented disparities in mental health care between minoritized ethnic/racial groups and non-Hispanic Whites. The findings of the report indicated differences in mental health utilization that were not solely attributable to personal preference. Instead, the report states, "Racial and ethnic minorities have less access to mental health services than do whites. They are less likely to receive needed care. When they receive care, it is more likely to be poor in quality" (U.S. Department of Health and Human Services, 2001, p. 3).

In response to the US Surgeon General report and subsequent research, several initiatives have been undertaken to eliminate mental health disparities. As identified in the Institute of Medicine's 2003 report, *Unequal Treatment*, initiatives have focused on two domains that contribute to barriers to access: system (health care/operations/legal/regulatory) and individual (patient/provider). System initiatives have included (1) mental health parity in the Affordable Care Act, (2) action plans to grow a diverse behavioral health workforce, (3) emphasis on integrating primary care and behavioral health settings for underserved minority populations, and (4) supporting research on the intersection between genetic and "zip" codes (i.e. economic and environmental factors) (Bussing & Gary, 2012; US Department of Health and Human Services, 2011; Institute of Medicine, 2003; Office of Disease Prevention and Health Promotion, n.d.). To address the individual contributing factors to disparities, mental health providers are called to make personal efforts to reach identified federal and regulatory goals. Such efforts include (1) regular continuing education to increase cultural humility and cultural comfort as well as decrease intellectual bias about various cultural groups; (2) cultivate diverse friendships to increase understanding of and sensitivity to the nuances of the realities of human difference; (3) increase community presence through volunteer activities or professional community service in the local community; and (4) engage in recruitment activities and mentorship for students from minoritized background to increase diverse representation in mental health workforce.

However, in the nearly two decades since the landmark Surgeon General publication and federal initiatives, the basic findings of mental health disparities of minoritized peoples have not much changed. In 2015, the Substance Abuse and Mental Health Services Administration (SAMHSA) published a chartbook with data from the National Survey on Drug Use and Health (NSDUH) on mental health service utilization among adults aged 18 or older within different racial/ethnic groups in the United States. The report highlights that African Americans or Blacks had a lower estimate of mental health care visits compared with White adults, regardless of gender, age, education level, income, and insurance status. The report also found that the overall pattern of differences was consistent in any mental health service use, prescription psychiatric medication use, and outpatient mental health service use. For inpatient mental health service use, however, Black adults had a higher estimate of service use than White adults. Additionally, respondents who identified as Black or African American reported having unmet mental health needs due to the cost of services (i.e. uninsured or underinsured) (45.4%), low perceived need (24.5%), prejudice/discrimination (25.3%), structural barriers, (31.6%), and not believing the services will help (5.3%).

The findings from the 2015 SAMHSA chartbook are consistent with the literature on the help-seeking behaviors of African Americans, further indicating structural barriers including financial constraints, lack of available services, and lack of awareness of culturally specific problems or racism/discrimination by health care providers (Holden, McGregor, Blanks, & Mahaffey, 2012; Matthews, Corrigan, Smith, & Aranda, 2006; Pieterse, Todd, Neville, & Carter, 2012; Ward, Clark, & Heidrich, 2009; Williams, Neighbors, & Jackson, 2008). Research has also elaborated on the determinants of specific cultural barriers influencing help-seeking behaviors of members of the Black community, including high levels of cultural mistrust in the mental health service system, fear of hospitalizations/being institutionalized, high levels of stigma, negative attitudes toward efficacy of treatment, preference for providers who are similar to their ethnic/racial background, and reliance on religious and other informal coping behaviors (Bowen-Reid & Harrell, 2002; Bradford, Newkirk, & Holden, 2009; Hammond, 2010; Holden et al., 2012; Scott, McCoy, Munson, Snowden, & McMillen, 2011; Townes, Cunningham, & Chavez-Korell, 2009; Utsey, Giesbrecht, Hook, & Stanard, 2008; Ward et al., 2009).

Despite health disparities being of national concern, current literature suggests that persisting attitudes/beliefs and system issues continue to interfere with members of the Black community utilizing mental health services. The complexities previously identified warrant consideration of more tailored strategic initiatives to eliminate disparities. Strategic advocacy efforts can create this shift both on the individual level as well as systems level.

Develop Interventions, Strategies, and Potential Allies to Enact Change

As highlighted previously, the confounding social, environmental, and cultural variables that impact help-seeking behaviors in the Black community are systemic and individual. The traditional medical model for treatment (i.e. the "black box" paradigm) is incompatible with the identified help-seeking behaviors of Black clients. The black box paradigm is the systemic ideology and practice that when people get sick, they go to treatment (the black box), they are "fixed," and then they are discharged. The problem with this paradigm is that it relates dysfunction (i.e. feeling unwell) to an outcome (i.e. seek treatment, follow prescribed remedy, return to activities of daily living) without considering the impact of intervening factors such as social and environmental variables (i.e. cultural mistrust of medical institutions, accessibility of services or recommended treatments, etc.).

A shift away from the "black box" paradigm of mental health services is needed for addressing unique barriers to access for members of the Black community. Clinicians, then, would be better able to serve the Black community by taking a public health approach. Such an approach would be multifaceted and calls you to be a presence in the environment to promote health and wellness. In doing so you will be able to eliminate overpathologizing clients and client communities and create a broader range of responses to powerful health predictors: social and economic factors. A public health approach may also effectively reduce cultural mistrust of the mental health care system. Research suggests that when providers are learning about and engaging in the communities served, they are better able to provide fair and just services. Professionals, then, need to integrate themselves and their expertise into the community to promote population health versus waiting for people to seek services.

Another consideration for being in the role of advocate is navigating the potential for paternalism, especially when a provider outside an oppressed community acts on behalf of that community (Toporek & Williams, 2006). By increasing awareness of intentions and motives as well as their place of privilege based on social class, educational opportunities, race, gender, or other attributes, the provider can moderate the conditions under which advocacy is enacted. Such a stance conveys respect, dignity, and responsibility for both the individuals and the communities that are being served. You can use your expertise to eliminate barriers to care and increase conscientiousness in how you engage and intervene within the Black community.

Interventions to address culture-specific barriers

Effective interventions to directly address culture-specific barriers including cultural mistrust, fear of hospitalizations/being institutionalized, stigma, negative attitudes toward the efficacy of treatment, and reliance on religious and other informal coping behaviors include:

- Collaborating with the spiritual/religious leaders to discuss mental health in the context of faith;
- Developing and facilitating workshops in places of business in the community (i.e. barber shops, beauty stores/salons, etc.);
- Creative uses of technology by developing online forums or meeting groups.

Interventions to address system barriers

To address specific problems of racism/discrimination by health care providers and clients' preference for providers from similar backgrounds, clinicians can consider actions that assure inclusion and equal opportunity in the organization or even educational institutions. Such actions can include:

- Expand and strengthen strategic partnerships with diverse affinity organizations, professional associations, and educational institutions to perform recruitment outreach focusing on promoting workforce diversity;
- Identify barriers to the recruitment, retention, and advancement of diverse providers;
- Increase diversity in leadership by aggressively promoting and communicating leadership development and mentoring programs to historically disenfranchised employees;
- Implement employee dialog sessions upon request and as needed to address specific, cultural, diversity and inclusion, and employee engagement topics;
- Deliver cultural competency, unconscious bias/implicit association, diversity and inclusion training;
- Leverage, support, and coordinate with community stakeholders;
- Develop an organizational strategic plan for diversity and inclusion and issue an annual performance report on progress made on the strategic plan;
- Employ strategies that aim to attract and empower broader, emerging aspects of diversity to counter negative perceptions about mental health services in the Black community.

Implement and Assess the Impact of the Strategic Advocacy Plan

After framing the problem and identifying intervention strategies, the implementation should follow a clear set of objectives and priorities (see Table 3.2). The advocate or consultant can then

Table 3.2 Sample Advocacy Plan

Organization Guiding Principle: provide outstanding, culturally competent services to consumers.

Identified Problem: low rating on consumer experience survey indicating perceived discrimination from staff and providers.

Goal: reduce the frequency of microaggressions that occur against consumers by agency staff, providers, and administrators in the mental health clinic.

Desired Outcomes:

Consumers: will be engaged in treatment services evidenced by the decrease in missed opportunity/no-show rate and increase in consumer experience rating.

Staff and Providers: will report increased cultural comfort in addressing culture-specific concerns of consumers.

Administrators/Managers: will lead efforts to increase cultural competency, decrease unconscious bias/implicit association, and implement patient-centered, cultural-oriented care standards.

Actions

1. Administrators will complete readings and online course on Microaggressions (www.lynda.com/Leadership-Management-tutorials/Microaggressions/664802/755475-4.html) in the next 30 days.
2. Administrators will complete reading of *White Fragility* by Robin DiAngelo and *Race Talk* and *Microaggressions in Everyday Life* by Derald Wing Sue and discuss reflections in leadership meeting by the end of the second quarter.
3. 30% of staff and providers will complete three hours of cultural competency, unconscious bias/implicit association, and diversity and inclusion training by the end of the first quarter. 70% of staff and providers to complete training by the end of the third quarter. 100% trained by the end of the fiscal year (FY).
4. Implement standardized agency-wide diversity and inclusion performance elements and standards in all employee performance plans.
5. Develop a Diversity and Inclusion Committee with agency and community members to consider diversity and inclusion matters impacting the provision of services.

(continued)

Table 3.2 (Continued)

Development Success Factors
Timeline: FY 2020–2021
Indicators of Success: leaders reported increased confidence and competence to initiate and engage in culturally sensitive dialogs with supervised employees and consumers. Frequency of initiating conversations about diversity/microaggressions with supervised employees, peers, and non-departmental staff increased. Staff and providers identify at least three occurrences of microaggressions occurring within the clinic and what was done to address the situation. Leaders seek feedback from consumers about their progress on the implemented action plan.

guide and inspire others to achieve results and improve organizational effectiveness, efficiency, and inclusion. Additionally, the mental health advocate defines evaluation criteria, specifies data to be gathered, develops systems for collecting and sharing data on progress towards achieving objectives, and takes calculated risks to accomplish change objectives and empowers others to do the same. While a clinician may be driven by results in advocacy efforts, it is also important for advocacy activities to foster accountability to the Black community. In other words, actions taken on behalf of the Black community must be in service to the community's overall health and well-being. In this way, the actions and activities employed by the clinician instill community trust while accomplishing the goal. Clinicians can then ensure compliance to evidence-based practices in the provision of services, and hold themselves and team members accountable for measurable, high quality, timely, and cost-effective results.

Summary

Mental health disparities continue to be a barrier to services for members of the Black community. The structural and culture-specific factors that contribute to disparities require strategic and persistent advocacy. Mental health providers possess the expertise to be powerful advocates beyond the treatment room. Developing a focused plan that leverages resilience, empowerment, and change strategies within the health care system and in the Black community will allow for the disruption of barriers and improved population health.

PART II
Implementing Culturally Responsive Care

Chapter 4	Assessment and Diagnosis of Race-Based Stress	65
Chapter 5	Engaging in Race Talk and Addressing Microaggressions in Therapy	85
Chapter 6	Culturally Responsive Interventions	115

CHAPTER 4
Assessment and Diagnosis of Race-Based Stress

Introduction

In its simplest form, assessment is used as a basis for identifying problems, planning interventions, evaluating and/or diagnosing, and informing clients and stakeholders. The practice of assessment entails the collection of information in order to identify, evaluate, and address the concerns of clients. It is noteworthy that providers attend to client–provider communication, notions of stigma, and cultural mistrust to minimize the negative affect such phenomenon can have on clinical judgment, the therapeutic relationship, and the types of diagnostic inferences made during the clinical interview. The integration of ethical, multiculturally competent assessment, formulation, and diagnosis necessitates the consideration of subjective evaluation of cultural, social, and environmental context. Such consideration requires the evaluator to not only utilize means/methods to measure symptoms or conditions, but the influences and effects of disease and health interventions on quality of life as well.

Effective assessment of an individual's perception of their life, within the context of the culture and value systems in which they live, is integral for accurate intervention. Inattentiveness to cultural considerations in the interview may engender over-identification or under-identification of psychiatric disorders across cultural groups or inadvertently promote stereotypes that impair clinical decision making (Alcantara & Gone, 2014). In the absence of more substantive sociocultural contextualization, clinicians may commit a false overgeneralization or impose Western psychiatric categories on other cultural groups without evidence or their cross-cultural validity.

Assessment instruments, structured, and semi-structured interview measures have been developed to address unintentional biases in the interview/assessment process. However, an instrument is only as "woke" as its developer. Through the decades of advocacy on the importance of diversity and inclusion in the provision of mental health services, practitioners and researchers have made gains in developing interview process and measures that assist in assessing a person's quality of life and overall well-being. The *Diagnostic and Statistical Manual of Mental Disorders'* (5th ed., American Psychiatric Association, 2013a) Cultural Formulation Interview (CFI) is one such example. However, this structured interview, while comprehensive, does not directly address the experience and impact of racial discrimination on a person's well-being. This is a significant limitation that may perpetuate institutionalized barriers to effective treatment for persons of color.

In the role of assessor or evaluator, you will do well to have an assessment practice that is sensitive to the nuances of the realities of human difference. Your capacity to understand a theory of difference can allow for more accurate identification of problems, diagnoses, and plan interventions. Consequently, you will be better able to empower clients because you are using cultural and personal factors relevant to their sense of self in the therapy work. In this chapter, we will present tools for effective assessment of race-based stress. We will also provide a model of conceptualizing mental health symptomology, quality of life concerns, and diagnostic considerations.

Exploring Psychometrics of the Self

Considerations of multiculturally competent assessment typically focus on determining the appropriate measures or methods that are generalizable to minoritized populations, language competencies of clients, and the appropriateness of diagnostic categories for cultural minority groups. It is also critical that practitioners pursue the understanding of the "psychometrics of the self." This concept, coined by Cimbora and Krishnamurthy (2018), implores providers to reflect on their implicit perceptions, reactions, biases, beliefs, values, assumptions, and areas of ignorance (blind spots that are tied to one's sense of self as an individual). Consequently, this examination brings better awareness of the impact our identities have on clinical work and allows for a more accurate assumption of who the client actually is. Such examination may allow for more creative responses and interventions for our clients by bringing into focus the ways in which the strengths and resiliencies inherent in identities inform, transform, and can also be distorted by distress and dysfunction (Brown, n.d.). Mental health providers, then, have better awareness of what they represent to their clients and what those clients represent to them. Inaccurate evaluations of self and fluctuations in the presentation of self to the client (e.g. either from session to session or from client to client), increase the likelihood that providers will impose a Western-based, medically oriented perspective on clients, whereby missing the nuances afforded by the client's subjective cultural realities.

As an example, let's take a look at a dialogue between Dr. Francis, a White cis-male therapist, and James, a Black cis-male client.

> James: It's just always on my mind whenever I'm in my car. I think it has to do in part with my being so involved with educating the young black men on what to do if they are stopped by the police. I feel so on edge. It wears on me all the time.
>
> Dr. Francis: I can hear it in your voice and see it in your body language. You seem weary just talking about this. I am wondering how this experience is also affecting your home and work life.
>
> James: I don't really talk about it at home. They already know what it's like to drive while Black. At work [chuckles], we steer clear of any conversation about race. It just gets too intense and I'm always the one trying to make them

see sense! They want to make it all about how "it wouldn't have happened if they just would have complied," and crap like that. But when I call out their White privilege, they get mad and make it seem like I'm racist.

Dr. Francis: I can understand that being upsetting. But let's get back to understanding how you're feeling on edge all the time. Can you describe more of the symptoms?

James: I mean, I just feel tense like I can't relax. I have to constantly be aware of where I am and how others are reacting to me being there.

Dr. Francis: Ok. Ok. Now we're getting somewhere. When you start feeling this tension, this hyperawareness, what goes through your mind? What thoughts come up?

James: I dunno. I just feel uneasy, like they think I'm a threat because I'm a tall Black man.

Dr. Francis: Ok. So, what else? If people think you are a threat, what does that mean to you?

James: ... It means I'm not safe because they're going to make an issue about me just existing in the space. If I move too quick, or speak too loud, or look too long ... it's always a problem to them.

Dr. Francis: I see. It makes sense to me then, why you would feel uneasy. It's what you're thinking! What you're saying to yourself, about yourself. It seems to me that you are using a sort of thinking filter here that distorts reality. And, in doing so, you're the one sitting in the angst and distress. It's not the environment or the people in your immediate surroundings. It's how you're thinking about it and them. And, my best guess is, this sort of thinking habit you have is developed from a skewed sense of self. So, that's the bad news. The good news, is now that we've identified it, we can change it!

The exchange between Dr. Francis and James exemplifies a professional attempting to apply a therapy modality to a client's experience. Though well meaning, and perhaps appropriately applying the intervention, Dr. Francis' assessment of the concern excluded James's subjective cultural reality. This exchange also raises questions about Dr. Francis' awareness of himself as a cultural being, his privileges as a White cis-male, and his implicit perceptions, reactions, biases, and assumptions. It may be assumed that Dr. Francis, in continuing his treatment planning, may be imposing his world view and perspective on James under the guise of psychological science. If so, Dr. Francis would be violating ethical standards and best practices in standards of care.

Practices for Exploring the Psychometrics of the Self

The following tasks, activities, and exercises have been informed by the literature (Baca & Smith, 2018; Hook, Davis, Owen, & DeBlaere, 2017; Pope, Sonne, Greene, & Vasquez, 2006) to include a developmental, multiculturally oriented perspective. The purpose of these exercises is to encourage a mindful awareness of the complex, and at times messy, intrapersonal and interpersonal engagements that exists in real life, how we respond to them, and the need for openness, honesty, courage, and constant questioning. However, the practices presented are not exhaustive. It is also encouraged that providers actively engage in supervision, therapy, and consultation to become more accurate self-evaluators.

Questions for Self-Reflection

- Have you had experience trusting those who are very different from you? How has this impacted your life, personally and professionally?
- Generally, are you too hard on yourself? Too easy on yourself (e.g., typically finding ways to avoid feedback and self-reflection)?
- Do you get "tired" or "bored" with some people and not others?
- With whom do you become avoidant?

- Do you "tolerate" some people?
- Do you find yourself "biting your tongue" with certain people?
- When have you found yourself using a tone that is patronizing or infantilizing with people?
- Whose strengths do you celebrate?
- With whom do you share your warmth and affection?
- When do you find yourself saying things that are harsh, sarcastic, and cynical?
- During your professional training/practice, what were some of the negative stories you were told/taught (implicitly or explicitly) about various cultural groups?
- Have you ever felt jealous of a client?
- Have you ever regretted bringing up a topic, disclosed something, or taken a stance? If so, what was it, and why did you regret it?
- During your professional training/practice, in what ways, if any, could openness, directness, and honesty be a liability? What, if anything, could not be questioned?
- Have you ever blushed or become embarrassed when you were in a therapy or evaluation with a client? Why?
- During your professional training/practice, what were some negative past experiences with individuals from different cultural groups?
- What are some of your own internalized, personal struggles with your cultural identity(ies) or cultural beliefs, values, and attitudes?
- What, if anything, could a client say or do to you that would be uncomfortable or embarrassing to you during the session?
- What, if anything, could a client say or do to you that you'd be uncomfortable or embarrassed putting in the client's chart?

- Have you ever worked with a client you hated? If so, could you work effectively with that client?
- If there are certain kinds of clients who make you uncomfortable, how would you describe them? How, if at all, does your discomfort affect your ability to work effectively with them? To what extent is your discomfort acknowledged or reflected in your notes?

Creating an intentional reflective practice increases self-validity and self-reliability as a mental health provider. In doing so, we as professionals can create a stable treatment environment that is responsive to fluctuations in client presentations as well as accurately assess differences between clients. However, reflection is only part of maintaining competence in assessment and evaluation. Using the awareness garnered from reflective practices, professionals can neutralize the intellectual, emotional, and relational components that maintain biases and increase professional liability. Hook et al. (2017) recommend the following such practices:

- Address the intellectual component of bias (i.e. stereotypes, overgeneralizations, and confirmation biases) by doing research, thinking, reflecting, and journaling.
- Address the emotional component of bias (i.e. anger, fear, suspicion, etc.) by exploring deepest thoughts and feelings about cultural groups you may hold bias towards. Utilize consultation, supervision, and/or therapy to assist in such exploration.
- Address the relational component of bias (i.e. avoidance of cultural groups) by developing positive relationships with member(s) of that group.

What Exactly Are We Assessing and Why?

Existing literature and research have established statistically significant relationships between perceived experiences with racism and a range of psychiatric and emotional reactions including adjustment, stress reaction, and mood and anxiety disorders (Carter, 2009; Williams et al., 2018). However, the literature also suggests that mental health professionals may not be adequately incorporating considerations of race, culture, racism, and discrimination in evaluations. This lack of consideration may be due to limited understanding or guidance in assessing and addressing the unique lived experiences of racial minorities.

To further complicate matters, racial encounters are often inexplicable and are not often discussed with mental health professionals. The lack of disclosure from clients may be due to lack of a shared language about race, culture, and discrimination. However, it has also been noted that racial encounters may not be discussed within affected communities or family groups in much detail. Whether or not this behavior is attributable to external factors or learned coping habits, mental health professionals have a duty to accurately assess strengths, liabilities, and dysfunction impacting the lives of clients. In doing so, providers must consider and critically assess client self-definitions, client-context (i.e. physical and psychological settings and environments that clients are immersed in), and apply evidenced-based concepts of distress and dysfunction, like race-based stress, to best serve their clients.

Carter and Forsyth (2009) and Carter (2007) provide a framework to best assess and conceptualize race-based stress and race-based traumatic stress, highlighting that distress is an outcome of exposure to racial discrimination, racism, and discrimination in general. First, the authors provide a distinction between stress and traumatic stress which has significance when determining the presence of pathology or disorders. Stress is defined as the appraisal of an event as positive, unwanted, negative, and/or taxing that requires one to adapt or cope in some way. The authors distinguish trauma as a more severe form of stress that circumvents a person's ability to cope. Further still, traumatic stress is a form of stress resulting from emotional pain as opposed to a life-threatening event or a series of events as the core stressor. The distinction between stress and trauma is important in planning for the most effective interventions. For example, the experience of stress may be best addressed using emotional regulation and interpersonal effectiveness skills. Trauma reactions and experiences may be better managed using distress tolerance skills. Choosing the best intervention strategies will be further presented in Chapter 6. At the assessment and diagnosis stage of mental health care, you will do well to be able to understand and articulate differences between the experience of stress and trauma.

In using the definitions and distinctions between stress and trauma, Carter (2007) defines race-based stress and trauma reactions as *racial encounters that must be sudden, unexpected, and emotionally painful*. This is the first tier to be met for accounting for trauma reactions. How encounters with racism are experienced depends on many factors associated with an individual's background, health, and cognitive processing. The person who interprets and appraises his racial encounter as extremely negative (emotionally painful), sudden, and uncontrollable, may exhibit signs and symptoms associated with the stress and possible trauma of racism. Reliance on a dispositional (i.e. intrapsychic) approach may hold your client responsible for situational factors outside her or his control. Employing the notion of injury may better capture the external violations and assaults inherent in racism/race-based encounters that create stress, distress, and trauma for clients. In doing so, providers are better able to assess and identify reactions that integrate the situational (external) and dispositional (internal) elements in the context of an individual's life history and experiences, including racism.

To increase validity and reliability of assessing for the mental health effects of racism and racial discrimination, it is useful to have types/classes of racism rather than using broad social definitions or systemic descriptions. Carter (2007) proposed the following three types of racism for assessing race-based stress: racial harassment (i.e. often indirect and avoidant including barring access, exclusion, withholding information, etc.), racial discrimination, (i.e. typically hostile and direct, including verbal and physical assaults, hostile work environment, and being profiled), and discriminatory harassment (i.e. aversive and hostile including isolation at work, denial of promotion, question of qualifications, etc.). Being able to assess for and recognize these classes of racism further empowers the professional and the client to delineate the racial encounter beyond calling it racism/discrimination and better understand the negative, and at times lasting, impact on mental health. In essence you will be able to create specific language around the unique experience and implement more precise and targeted interventions.

In their research on race-based stress, Carter and colleagues have found that there are specific symptom clusters that clients report following negative racial encounters. The reports of symptom clusters allow clinicians to establish diagnostic criteria to classify the impact on mental health and well-being. For example, criteria have been defined to include the reporting of two or three symptoms (i.e. reactions that are arousal or hypervigilance, intrusion, or re-experiencing an avoidance or numbing). Other symptoms expressed are important but not necessary for determining race-based trauma injury, including depression, anger, physical reactions, and low self-esteem. The severity of the impact on functioning can then lead to formal mental health diagnoses and effective treatment planning.

One particular tool that may be useful in the assessment of racial trauma is the University of Connecticut Racial/Ethnic Stress and Trauma Scale (UnRESTS). This semi-structured interview allows the mental health professional to facilitate conversation with the client about experiences with racism while building rapport (Williams et al., 2018; Williams, Pena, & Mier-Chairez, 2017). This instrument provides professionals with specific questions and instructions to navigate the assessment of racially charged topics. UnRESTS's semi-structured nature gives providers flexibility to follow-up to get more detailed descriptions of experiences. The format of the interview is broken into sections to include introduction to the interview, racial and ethnic identity development, experiences of direct overt racism, experiences of racism by loved ones, experiences of vicarious racism, and experiences of covert racism (Williams et al., 2018; 2017). Lastly, the instrument also provides guidance for making a diagnosis of post-traumatic stress disorder (PTSD) by aligning information gathered with the current DSM-5 criteria. We believe this is a crucial instrument to assess and treat Black clients for experiences of racial discrimination.

Assessment Instruments

The use of testing instruments/tools during assessment should be in an effort to obtain a more complete picture of the types of verbal, perceptual, and motor behaviors clients engage in their everyday lives. Every reaction to test stimuli or questions is a projection of the private world and personal characteristics of the client. Integration of data with interpretations (that are relevant to the client) constructs the assessment.

There has been a compendium of instruments developed over the past 10–12 years that measure perceived racism and/or discrimination. Understanding the available measures is important for assessing and comparing racism/discrimination across health care environments, documenting the presence or degree of racism/discrimination, and measuring changes in levels subsequent to interventions (Kressin, Raymond, & Manze, 2008). Commonly used instruments to assess exposure to racism and its impact are:

>   Race-Based Traumatic Stress Symptom Scale (RBTSSS)
>   General Ethnic Discrimination Scale (GEDS)
>   The Racial Microaggressions Scale modified (RMAS)
>   Schedule of Racist Events (SRE)
>   Racism and Life Experience Scales (RaLES)
>   Experiences of Discrimination (EOD)
>   Perceived Racism Scale (PRS)
>   Everyday Discrimination Scale (EDS)
>   Perceived Ethnic Discrimination Questionnaire (PEDQ)
>   Multidimensional Inventory of Black Identity (MIBI)
>   Index of Race-Related Stress – Brief Version (IRRS-B)
>   Racism Experiences Stress Scale (EXP-STR)

While the above instruments have been developed to assist in the assessment of the impact of racial discrimination, they are not without critiques and limitations. For example, few measures are theoretically based, with most assessing only general dimensions of racism and focused specifically on the experiences of African American patients (Atkins, 2014). Additional measures are needed for detailed assessments of perceived discrimination that are relevant for a wide variety of racial/ethnic groups. The literature also recommends future research and instrument development to assess how racism/discrimination affects health care decision making and treatments offered.

We recommend that if professionals choose to use an instrument to assess for race-based stress/trauma, special care is taken to consider the psychometric properties of the measure. In essence, the measure chosen should assess whether racist/discriminatory events/actions occurred and the extent of impact on the functioning of the individual experiencing them. Additional instrument measures can also address whether the racist/discriminatory events/actions experiences affect the individual's interaction with his or her health care provider, client's view or acceptance of the provider's treatment recommendations, or the provider's offer of care.

Making the Case for DSM Diagnosis(es)

Although the presented framework for race-based stress and trauma and the highlighted assessment instruments provide conceptual clarity, it is important to acknowledge that the DSM-5, does not include consideration of the racial-cultural context in listed diagnoses, particularly PTSD (Carter, 2007; Carter & Forsyth, 2009; Williams et al., 2018). The criteria for a diagnosis of PTSD requires an index trauma event, including either exposure to actual or threatened death, serious injury, or sexual violence that can either be experienced directly or witnessed by the individual, learning the event occurred to a family member or close friend, or repeated exposure to aversive details of the event (American Psychiatric Association, 2013a). A trauma stressor, as conceptualized in the

DSM-5, does not include racial discrimination events, especially if there is no direct evidence of physical violence. Therefore, a Black client who reports experiencing a negative racial encounter, and demonstrates symptoms consistent with PTSD, would likely have the severity of their symptoms dismissed because the event would not be considered catastrophic enough to meet DSM-5 criteria for the diagnosis (Carter & Forsyth, 2009). Researchers have called for the inclusion of racial discrimination events to be recognized as legitimate trauma stressors, thereby being acknowledged as contributable to an authentic, diagnosable, treatable form of PTSD.

To make the case for a diagnosis(es) using DSM-5 criteria, understanding the sequelae race-based stress and trauma is also important in knowing what to ask and how to conceptualize information gathered from interviews and assessment instruments into a diagnostic formulation. As discussed previously, DSM-5 definition of a trauma event will need to be broadened beyond a simple, circumscribed event such as death, threatened death, serious injury, or actual or threatened sexual violence. Instead, it is important to acknowledge discrimination and racism as a complex trauma experience arising from repeated or prolonged exposure to assaults on the personhood and integrity of the victim (Williams et al., 2018). The impact of these experiences is best understood using with the stress sensitization hypothesis that suggests repeated exposure to external and endogenous stressors results in the progressive amplification of a response. In other words, every personal or vicarious encounter with racism (i.e. overt, covert, and cultural) contributes to a more insidious, chronic experience of stress. Over time, the accumulation of stress inflicts psychological and physiological injuries, increasing the likelihood of a pathological response to future exposure to negative racial encounters and prevents the natural abatement of symptoms (Harkness, Hayden, & Lopez-Duran, 2015; Williams, et al., 2018). In this way, ongoing exposure to racism and discrimination reshapes individuals' sense of themselves, their identity and identity group, and their place in the world. Exposure may also manifest in distressing memories, intrusive thought or ruminations, distress over reminders of encounters, avoidance behaviors, depression, anxiety, feeling unsafe, hypervigilance, poor sleep, difficulty concentrating, anger, guilt, low self-esteem, and even suicidal or homicidal ideation.

Compounding the subsequent psychological distress of racism further, the literature has indicated that there are social costs for sharing personal experiences of racism or discrimination including being perceived as less likable, viewed as a complainer, and accused of attempting to avoid personal responsibility (Williams et al., 2018). In addition to the negative mental health impact of racism, victims are also then burdened with the dissonance between their personal reality of encountering racial stressors and conflicting social messages that indicate racism is not a valid explanation for their experiences. Mental health providers can perpetuate the experience of invalidation by rigidly adhering to the DSM criteria that do not account for the psychopathological impact of racial discrimination. It is therefore incumbent on you to consider, conceptualize, and articulate how racial trauma, whether direct or indirect, has similar behavioral health consequences to those for individuals who have experienced traumatic events such as death, threatened death, serious injury, or actual or threatened sexual violence.

Case Example 1

Mr. Davis is a middle-aged male who identifies as African American. He presented to a community clinic for a mental health assessment. When Mr. Davis meets with the clinician, he described increased irritability and stress and feeling overwhelmed with life. He described starting a new job where he is the only African American and only person of color in the office. He further described feeling "paranoid" around his co-workers and increased difficulty completing tasks at work. Given Mr. Davis' report of symptoms and current psychosocial stressors, the assessing clinician utilized the UnRESTS semi-structured interview to gather more detailed information about Mr. Davis' racial identity, history, and current experiences of direct and covert racism and racial discrimination. Using the questions and prompts in the UnRESTS, Mr. Davis reported that during his first week at work, he was getting into his car in the parking lot when two men came up behind him, slamming him into the side of his car, pushing his head down on the roof, and putting "something" on the side of his neck, while stating "Run yo pockets fool!" Mr. Davis described being terrified in the moment and attempted to comply with the assailants. After what felt like "forever," Mr. Davis stated the two assailants started laughing and released him. Still afraid, Mr. Davis turned and saw two of his new White co-workers laughing and stating "welcome to the team bro." Mr. Davis then became angry and pushed one of the co-workers declaring that what they did was not funny. Mr. Davis then stated the co-workers began to mock him with statements like "What? You can't handle a joke," "You should be used to that coming from the inner city," and "Don't be so uppity." The co-workers then continued to joke and mock Mr. Davis's reaction before walking away. Since that incident, Mr. Davis learned that there was another co-worker involved who video recorded the event and shared it around the office. Mr. Davis made a complaint to his direct supervisor, whose response was:

> It was just a prank. You're taking it too seriously. They didn't mean any harm. They were just trying to bond, don't take it personally. You're not one of those people who like to pull the race card because they're too sensitive, are you?

Over the following four months, Mr. Davis described increased distress at work, intrusive thoughts about the event, disturbed sleep, attempts to avoid all co-workers,

> hypervigilance, difficulty concentrating at work, increased startle response, self-blame, anxiety, and depression. After learning more of Mr. Davis' recent experiences following the event, the assessing clinician was able to use the UnRESTS to identify and confirm DSM-5 PTSD symptoms attributable to Mr. Davis' report of a racial trauma event.

It is also important to note that not all traumas result in a diagnosis of PTSD. The same can be said for race-based stress experiences. In such cases, you can still acknowledge the deleterious impact of racial stress on the Black client and then complete a differential diagnosis of other diagnoses or disorders. When the racial stress is not the primary focus, but still a significant factor on functioning, clinicians should consider DSM-5's Use of Other Specified and Unspecified Disorders, as well as Other Conditions That May Be a Focus of Clinical Attention (American Psychiatric Association, 2013a).

The Other Specified Trauma- and Stressor-Related Disorder category may be used with the client who reports symptoms of trauma with clinically significant distress, but full criteria is not met. This diagnosis allows the clinician to communicate the presence and impact of racial encounters by highlighting the reported symptoms, even when Criteria A of PTSD cannot be directly identified. For example, if a client describes symptoms of intrusive thoughts, mood reactivity, and distorted thoughts following repeated exposure to watching videos of Black people being killed by police, Criteria A of PTSD would not be met. Vicarious experiencing of racialized violence through media is specifically noted as not meeting criteria (American Psychiatric Association, 2013a). However, the client's psychological distress is clinically significant. In this case the diagnosis of Other Specified Trauma- and Stressor-Related Disorder, with a specifier of Race-based Traumatic Stress Reaction would be appropriate.

Being able to make a diagnosis is not only helpful in creating a shared language, but also validates the client concerns or presentation. In turn, clinicians and treatment teams will have a more accurate clinical picture. However, diagnoses may also be stigmatizing to the individual. It is important to make distinctions between clinically significant symptoms that indicate psychopathology, warranting a diagnosis and treatment, and not overpathologizing clients, especially when there are environmental and/or psychosocial elements that sustain distress. In such cases, the DSM-5's Other Conditions That May Be a Focus of Clinical Attention may be useful. More specifically, the conditions and problems under Other Conditions That May Be a Focus of Clinical Attention are not mental disorders but are meant to draw attention to the scope of additional issues that may be encountered in routine clinical practice and to provide a way for clinicians to document these issues (American Psychiatric Association, 2013a).

The conditions or problems that would best capture race-based stress reaction that have not resulted in other clinically significant symptoms are Social Exclusion or Rejection and Target of (Perceived) Adverse Discrimination or Persecution. Social Exclusion or Rejection category allows clinicians to document when social power imbalances create or result in recurrent social exclusion or rejection by others including bulling, teasing, intimidation, verbal abuse, or exclusion from activities of peers, co-workers, etc. (American Psychiatric Association, 2013a). Target of (Perceived) Adverse Discrimination or Persecution can be used when the client, based on their minoritized group membership or identity, reports experiences or perceived discrimination or persecution. Again, this category can be added to the diagnostic impression when experiences of racial discrimination warrant clinical attention. Carter's (2007) delineation of classes of racial encounters described previously (i.e. racial harassment, racial discrimination, and discriminatory harassment) align with both Social Exclusion or Rejection and Target of (Perceived) Adverse Discrimination or Persecution that warrant clinical attention. Clinicians are encouraged to give consideration to these diagnostic categories when completing diagnostic formulations when a clear mental health diagnosis is not present. It can also be useful in justifying a clinical treatment.

Case Example 2

Mrs Johnson is a 60-year-old Black woman who is seeking treatment for worsening depression and increasing stress. During the intake interview to establish care, she discloses a history of diagnosis and treatment of Major Depressive Disorder using both medications and psychotherapy interventions. Mrs Johnson endorsed symptoms consistent with a diagnosis of Major Depressive Disorder and relayed that her symptoms began to worsen approximately six weeks before the scheduled appointment. She was unable to identify any particular trigger but described increase responsibilities at home due to a change in her husband's health and difficultly managing new "wifely and grandmotherly duties." Mrs Johnson also described feeling more isolated at work following a "charged" conversation with her younger White co-workers about the removal of confederate monuments and statues. She distinctly recalls one of her co-workers calling her a racist, and stated that since Mrs Johnson lived through the civil rights movement, she should know better. The interviewer then administered the Perceived Ethnic Discrimination Questionnaire (PEDQ) and UnRESTS. Data for both measures indicated additional experiences with microaggressions, exclusion from social gatherings at work, cworkers withholding information, etc., which has led to increased experience of stress and loneliness. Although Mrs Johnson is experiencing racial stress, it does not meet the level of criteria for PTSD or Other Specified Trauma- and Stressor-Related Disorder. She does, however, meet criteria for Major Depressive Disorder, Recurrent, Moderate. Her experiences of race-based stress do appear to be a contributing factor to her depressive symptoms. It would then be appropriate to use Social Exclusion or Rejection to document the influences of such experiences on current symptomology and level of functioning.

Case Example 3

Mr. Warren is a 25-year-old African American gay cisgender male graduate student. He presented to the campus counseling center for a walk-in supportive counseling session. Mr. Warren disclosed to the therapist that he has been involved in the campus gay/straight alliance group called Prism. Mr. Warren described recent tensions in the group, particularly with their all-White student leadership. Specifically, he stated that recently he advocated for the replacing of the club logo with the new Pride flag, which incorporates the black and brown stripes to represent inclusion of LGBTQIA people of color. Mr. Warren stated he was passionate in his advocacy through highlighting the history of the exclusion of people of color from the LGBTQIA community. The response he received was surprising in that the leadership and some of the other White group members rejected his idea and the notion that the LGBTQIA community has been biased. Mr. Warrant then tried to argue his point but was then "accused of causing factions in the group" and that his proclamations were unnecessary and unhelpful. Since that time, he and other Prism members of color have been left off email announcements. Additionally, his ability to accurately/appropriately represent LGBTQIA to the public has been openly questioned by the group leadership. In response, Mr. Warren described feeling hurt, but also motivated to speak truth to power, even if it is to a group he feels "should already know." At this time, he reports some increase in stress but believes he is able to utilize adaptive coping skills to manage. Mr. Warren did not endorse any other mental health symptoms. The therapist validated his thoughts, feelings, experiences, and use of adaptive coping skills. Mr. Warren was also provided some psychoeducation about microaggressions. As the supportive therapy session closed, Mr. Warren expressed appreciation for the psychoeducation about microaggressions and relief that he "isn't the crazy one." Mr. Warren did not meet DSM–5 criteria for PTSD and did not endorse clinically significant distress that warrants any other diagnoses. In this case, use of Target of (Perceived) Adverse Discrimination or Persecution is appropriate for charting and billing purposes.

Summary

An overarching goal for addressing race-based stress in Black clients is to improve quality of life. To meet this goal, accurate assessment of mental health functioning and symptoms must include considerations of race and racial discrimination/harassment, and cumulative cultural traumas. Integrating appropriate assessment instruments can facilitate conversation in provider–client dyads and lead to accurate diagnostic formulation, case conceptualization, and effective treatment planning. Mental health professionals should also consider the psychometric of the self to identify and address potential biases that may impact the provision of mental care. It is recommended, then, that professionals establish intentional self-reflection into clinical practice as well as routine consultation or supervision.

CHAPTER 5
Engaging in Race Talk and Addressing Microaggressions in Therapy

Introduction

The idea of race is engrained in the fabric of American society. Historically, race has been conceptualized as the biological differences between people, identifying "Caucasians" as inherently superior to all other defined groups. That conceptualization has long been debunked by the scientific community. There is no agreement regarding what constitutes a particular race or how many "races" may exist. There is also no evidence that any group is superior to another. And yet, the idea of race is powerful and persistent, shaping basic relationships among people. In the US, the political economy of race has facilitated the unequal distribution of power, wealth, privilege, and land, mostly concentrating it in White society. This system of distribution (institutionalized racism) has been sustained at the macro level, and is often unacknowledged. Consequently, to name the existence of systemic racism in a context in which race is almost entirely denied creates a unique barrier in assessing and addressing its meaning and effects on individuals/ communities in the treatment context (Harries, 2014). In essence, we do not have a shared language to listen and exchange ideas about race, racism, Whiteness, and White privilege.

As practitioners, we may have received little, if any, training in self-awareness with respect to racism, and, therefore, have difficulty engaging others in conversations about race. Our clients' understanding and dialog about race will likely be significantly influenced by personal experiences with racism and pop culture, which are reflective of institutional racism in the dominant culture. Providers who are able to discuss and demonstrate a competency for race-related discourse may provide a liberating experience for Black clients. Engaging in race talk, then, is germane to the competent provision of mental health services in addressing race-based stress. In this chapter, we will present race talk as a multicultural competency skill set and provide tools and tips to develop and practice this skill in addressing race-based stress.

Understanding Race Talk and Microaggressions

As previously mentioned, race talk is a dialog or conversation about race, racism, Whiteness, and White privilege (Sue, 2016). It is more pervasive than ever in social discourse and discord. Race talk has no specific outcomes or objectives, but often is the expression of different perspectives, world views, and lived experiences. If discussants perceive their world view as being challenged or invalidated, race talk can shift to monologs in which participants restate, with greater intensity and conviction, their own positions. Consequently, engaging in racial dialogs can engender intense emotions, which can be perceived as threatening by participants. Due to the emotionally latent and personal nature of talking about race, there is potential for disastrous consequences if handled poorly by the facilitator or instigator. Review vignettes 1 through 3 for examples of race talk dialogs.

Vignette 1: The Wedding Reception

Whitney, an African American woman, attended the wedding of a close friend. At the reception dinner, she was seated with a couple mutual friends and several others whom she met for the first time at the wedding. Whitney was the only Black wedding attendee. The people at Whitney's table engaged in small talk while waiting for the next course to be served. During a lull in the conversation, Carol, a White woman, paid Whitney a compliment about her hair. Whitney thanked Carol for her compliment and then turned her attention to another conversation happening at the table. Carol then asked, "Whitney, how do you get your hair to be like that? It must take a long time." Whitney politely responded stating her natural hair allows for creative styling and it's well worth the time it takes to get it done. Carol then says, "It's so beautiful and different. Y'all just are so creative." In her mind, Whitney asked, "Different for who? And, who is 'yall'?" and attempted to remain polite by thanking Carol and turning her attention away. Carol then broken into the conversation awkwardly saying, "I'm sorry. I don't want to be rude. I never get a chance to ask these questions and I have always wondered how you people do your hair." Whitney, unsure of how to respond to the comment, took a breath and said, "What do you mean?" Carol then launched into her explanation, "I never get a chance to ask about Black hair and didn't want to come off rude or insensitive." Whitney's friend, then jumps in to say "Whitney is the best person to talk to. She never takes offense and is always willing to help." Attempting to remain calm, Whitney confronts Carol saying,

> Well ... it doesn't sound like you associate with many Black people. But, if you were so curious, I wonder why you never took the time to find out for yourself by researching it. There are tons of YouTube videos that provide much education about Black hair and haircare.

Carol then stated she never thought to watch videos, but that she does have Black friends but she didn't want to offend them by asking. Whitney then questioned Carol about asking her and if Whitney should feel offended. Coral, growing more incensed, then said, "Look, I didn't mean to make a big deal about this. This is why I never ask questions or bring things up. People are so easily offended by simple questions and then get defensive and call me a racist." Whitney then said, "Carol, playing the victim here does not help you. You were insensitive in expecting me to educate you as if that is my role." At this comment, another mutual friend jumped into the conversation to change the topic saying, "Hey guys, let's just talk about something else. Whitney, she didn't mean anything by asking. Just let it go."

Vignette 2: Trivia Night

Tim meets up with a group of friends for trivia night at the neighborhood bar. The group is a mix of men and women, and various ethnicities. Tim, who is of Asian descent, is close to the majority of people in the group. During a round of trivia a question about the name of a WNBA player comes up and the group has two minutes to submit their answer. The following dialog occurs:

> John (White, male): Aw man! Why couldn't it be a question about the NBA. I don't know the women players!
>
> Ashley (African American, female): Ugh! The name was on the tip of my tongue! Come on Mr. Sportsman John! You've got to know this! Just think for a moment!
>
> John: Calm down Ash. I don't know.
>
> Ashley: So, don't tell me to calm down. I just need you to help with the answer. You have got to know the name! She was that famous Sparks player ... the one that had been in the league since it started! Come on!

John: Geez, Ash! I don't know! Seriously! These are your people anyway.

Ashley: Excuse me? What's that supposed to mean?

John: You know. Aren't you a "root for anyone Black" type of girl?

Tim: That's not cool, John.

John: What? Aren't I right?

Ashley: Yea. You're right ... right-wing racist!

John: God! Here we go. Whenever a White person says anything about race, we're automatically racist. That's a very snowflake agenda, Ashley! I expected more from you.

Tim: [cutting off Ashley as she starts to respond] John, it did come off as a bit racist. That's like saying I should know every laundromat owner because I'm Asian and that you should know every mass murdering White kid because your White.

John: Whoa! Now I'm being ganged up on. You two are being racist now. And how dare you say I'm like those psychopaths!

From this point the conversation devolves into personal attacks and the group begins to argue and take sides.

Vignette 3: Spa Day

Julia and Val have been good friends for several years. During one of their regular spa day retreats, Val, a Dinè woman, shares with Julia, a woman of Arab descent, several negative experiences she had at work the previous week. After Val shared her experiences, Julia began to question why Val was so upset by the interactions.

Julia: Why get so upset about what they said? You're kind of making it a bigger issue than it really is.

Val: Wha? How can you say that? Why give these White women a pass for insulting me and making light of my heritage? It is a big deal.

Julia: I'm not saying you shouldn't be upset, but why stay upset about it? Just let it go. So what? They made some ignorant statements. Everybody does that from time to time.

Val: Why are you defending them? White people get a pass all the time. That's what is the problem with this country. No one wants to hold White people accountable.

Julia: Ok. So, I get you're upset but now I'm feeling a little offended. You sound a bit militant right now.

Val: Why would you feel offended?

Julia: Because I identify as White.

Val: Uh ... but your family is from Lebanon. How could you possibly be White? Your skin is olive and your hair and eyes are dark. Why would you think you're White?

Julia: I may not look White, but that's how I was raised. I mean, look, I'm not Black or Asian or Latino. I and my family were never accepted in those groups. When filling out forms there is never a box to check for Arab. I either have to choose White, Black, Asian, or Native. What other choice did I really have?

Val: But, do you really think of yourself as White? Do others treat you as White?

Julia: What does it mean do "others treat me as White"?

Val and Julia then began to discuss how they each came to understand themselves as racial cultural beings, especially by how their environments responded to them. Val was able to express the hurt caused by experiencing racism growing up and in her current workplace. Julia was better able to understand Val's anger and distrust of White institutions. Julia felt heard and understood by Val when sharing her experience of developing her racial identity within the social construct of the US. At the end of the spa day, both friends walked away feeling more connected and appreciative of their relationship.

As you may have noticed in the vignettes, the topic of race came up unexpectedly. Additionally, the initiating comments can be characterized as microaggressions. Microaggressions are everyday verbal, non-verbal, and environmental slights, snubs, or insults, whether intentional or unintentional to target persons based solely upon their marginalized group membership (Sue, 2010). They are often unconsciously delivered and can be characterized by communications that convey rudeness and insensitivity, and demean a person's racial heritage or identity, or exclude, negate, or nullify the psychological thoughts, feelings, or experiential reality of a person of color. Microaggressions are pervasive and automatic in daily conversations and interactions such that they are often dismissed and glossed over as being innocent and innocuous. As noted in previous chapters, the pervasiveness of microaggressions against members of the Black community contributes to poor physical and mental health.

In the therapy context, research indicates that 53% to 81% of clients report experiencing at least one microaggression in therapy (Owen et al., 2018). Clients' reports did not vary by racial-ethnic status. Owen et al. (2017) also found that 76% of the clients who experienced a microaggression in therapy also noted the therapist never addressed the incident. Research has linked lower client satisfaction, poor outcomes, and reports of poor working alliance to perceived and unresolved microaggressions in therapy (Owen et al., 2011; Owen et al., 2018). Given this data, it is a question of *when*, versus *if*, you may engage in a microaggression during the provision of therapy.

Though it may be common for racial dialogs to start with a microaggression occurring, whether in the therapy context or not, the literature suggests interracial and intergroup dialogs and interactions have positive benefits and evoke constructive changes among participants, leading to an expansion of critical consciousness. More specifically, according to Sue, (2016), racial dialogs have been shown to:

Increase racial literacy;

Expand the ability to critically analyze racial ideologies;

Increase ability to dispels stereotypes and misinformation about other groups;

Decrease intimidation and fear of differences;

Increase compassion for others;

Increase appreciation of people of all colors and cultures;

Create greater sense of belonging and connectedness with all groups.

With such contrasting outcomes to engaging in race talk, it is important to realize that *how* these dialogs are facilitated. Silencing and shutting down conversations only reinforce the idea that racial dialog is inappropriate (as seen in the Wedding Reception vignette). Allowing for intensely passionate monologs about defending one's experiential reality with no checks and balances may serve to reinforce negative perceptions or stereotypes of the "other" (exemplified in the Trivia Night vignette). However, if each party is willing to listen deeply, willing to "try on" another perspective, compassion and connection can happen (as seen in the Spa Day vignette). Therefore, race talk must be facilitated in such a way that participants can bear witness to lived realities other than their own, which may lead to corrective emotional experiences.

The ability to facilitate meaningful racial dialogs requires intentional self-reflection on your knowledge and attitudes, as well as commitment to seeking out education, consultation, and training experiences to improve understanding and effectiveness in working with client communities. Intentional self-reflection of your knowledge and attitudes is a starting place in developing race talk skills. In particular having an understanding of one's own racial identity influences comfort in the discussion of race(ism). Again, the construct of race not only implies a racial identity but also a sociohistorical position in society. An ecological understanding of one's self within the client community is needed. The exercise in Box 5.1 may prove illuminating for self-reflection on race within an ecological system.

Box 5.1 Reviewing the ADDRESSING Model

Review your responses to the ADDRESSING model and reflect on pride or shame issues of your identified racial ethnic group. For example, in some cultures, having a darker skin complexion might be a shame issue, whereas demonstrating artistry through the spoken word is a pride issue. It is important to emphasize that pride and shame issues are often socially constructed. When reflecting on such issues related to ADDRESSING elements, you should draw from multiple sources including but not limited to personal knowledge, interviewing family members or group members, books, films, and other cultural artifacts. For example, you may reflect on negative stories that were told about cultural groups from your family? What negative past experiences arise with individuals from various cultural groups? How are people with similar cultural identities portrayed in mass media? Where/how is your racial ethnic group represented in industry, social services, and politics? How, in the history of your culture, is your racial ethnic group represented?

After reflecting, continue self-exploration, focusing in on racial ethnic identities by writing responses to the following questions. Keep in mind that it may prove beneficial to share your reflections with trusted peers or supervisors for feedback.

> What aspects of your racial/ethnic identity do you embrace or reject?
>
> What cultural biases about your racial ethnic identity (positive and negative) have been transmitted to you from your family of origin? From your social network/community? From movies, books, music? From political influences? From law/legal contexts? From your professional training? Be sure to reflect/write on positive biases as they may result in patronization, over-identification, idealization, or failure to challenge and accept less than optimal behaviors because of one's cultural group.
>
> What are you most or least comfortable with in your racial/ethnic identity?
>
> What impact may pride/shame issues have on your ability to engage and facilitate race talk?

What Can Happen During Race Talk

As illustrated in the above vignettes, race talk is not contained in intellectual discussions in academic settings, but occurs in daily interactions with others in the world. It can be direct, indirect, innocuous, well-meaning, humorous, offensive, or malicious. It is in the fabric of our social discourse specifically because our reality is connected to the sociohistorical racial construct.

Reflection Point

Reflect on your last 24 hours. Where might you have observed/engaged in race talk? What were your reactions? How did you respond?

When engaging in race talk, awareness of your own discomfort is important as well as awareness of social norms that may influence participant behaviors, particularly when experiencing discomfort. For example, by and large, we are socialized to avoid public discourse on topics that may be offensive or cause discomfort. If such topics, like race and racism, cannot be avoided they should be discussed briefly and superficially as an objective, intellectual inquiry. To do otherwise would be impolite and divisive. There may also be an attempt to promote the social norm of a colorblind society. A colorblind society is problematic in that it emphasizes that race does not matter, only the character of a person matters, which further perpetuates aversive racism. Race talk not only clashes with the above social norms but can also expose power differentials between dominant group narrative about race and the less powerful counternarrative of the socially marginalized group (Sue, 2016). Vignette 4 illustrates these points.

Vignette 4

Megan and her family, who are African American, attended a jazz trio concert featuring a young, up-and-coming Black male pianist. The concert was held in an intimate recital room with seating for an audience of 75. Most of the audience were older and White. Megan and her family sat in the first row, nearest the pianist. At the end of the concert, Megan began to collect her belongings when another audience member, an older White woman, initiated conversation with Megan. The audience member remarked how she enjoyed the concert and then asked Megan if she was related to the pianist. Megan paused before responding then stated, "No. Why would you ask that?" The audience member then gave a nervous chuckle and responded saying "Oh. I just thought that maybe you were related. That's all." In response, Megan again asked the woman why she would think they were related. The woman, beginning to become uncomfortable, stated that she was just asking a simple question and that there was no reason to be upset. At this point, Megan was becoming more irritated and asked "What? How can you tell me to not be upset when you make such ignorant assumptions about us? You think all Black people are related? Are we still doing this in 2020?" As Megan spoke, her voice began to rise and the woman began to hurry away from the family. As Megan's partner attempted to console her, Megan continued to speak in a raised voice expressing her disbelief at the woman's comment. Other audience members skirted around the family, kept their eyes averted, and shook their heads as they passed.

Additionally, participants' racial and ethnic identities influence reactions and responses to race talk. White people may experience stress related to racial encounters. This phenomenon is termed White fragility. DiAngelo (2018) describes White fragility as a "protective pillow" of White privilege that insulates and builds White expectations for racial comfort while at the same time lowering the ability to tolerate racial stress. When confronted with nonWhite lived experiences of race and racism, White participants may experience intolerable amounts of stress and may engage in defensive moves that reinstate White racial equilibrium, including outward emotional displays, becoming argumentative/combative, becoming silent, or leaving the stress-inducing situation (DiAngelo, 2018). People of color's reaction and response to race talk may be marked by strong emotions, internal conflict, and at times evoke personal attacks. It is often the case that racial dialogs are triggered by a microaggression. When a microaggression occurs, whether it be personally experienced or witnessed, people of color have reported intense uncomfortable emotions such as anger, anxiety, and invalidation. Intrapersonal conflict may arise in deciding if and how to respond, as well as concerns about retaliation from the environment.

When to Initiate Race Talk in Therapy

In the therapy context, race talk can arise when clients mention a cultural belief, value, or some other aspects of their cultural heritage. It can unfold naturally over the course of therapy rather than in response to a specific set of rules therapists must adhere to in therapy. There is no one right way to engage or facilitate race talk. It may be easier to identify the "wrong" way to engage. Nonetheless, there are specific considerations, guidelines, and approaches to employ to increase the likelihood that the dialog can lead to an expansion of critical consciousness and sense of well-being.

Identify Your Own Racial Identity and What It Means to You

After engaging in the reflection exercises in Chapter 1, you may have articulated your racial/ethnic identity. The importance of understanding yourself as a racial-cultural being cannot be overstated. Humble reflection and taking ownership of the ways you have been influenced by existing racial constructs of society can help you navigate race talk in therapy, especially when addressing race-based stress.

Furthermore, clients may project their perception, expectations, and biases on you due to the racial/ethnic group they believe you belong to. Your understanding of yourself as a racial-cultural being together with your practice of cultural humility will allow you to navigate race talk opportunities in therapy. Follow the exchange below between Nicole, a Black female therapist, and Daniel, a 74-year-old White male. As you read, look for cultural opportunities for race talk and how the therapist responds.

Nicole: So, how have you been Daniel?

Daniel: I've been managing. I still go to my VFW [Veterans of Foreign Wars] meetings and try to support the younger Vets. I'm still struggling financially. I've tried to get food stamps, but you know how the system works. They say they'll start you at $20 a week and then you have to wait and wait until they increase it. They only say that because of this [points and rubs forearm]. If it wasn't for this, I'd have no problem.

Nicole: [thinking Daniel is pointing out his liver spots, and assumes he is referring to ageism] You find you are being treated differently because of your age?

Daniel: No! Because of this [points again at forearm]. Because I'm White! It's reverse discrimination. But they do work and get money from the government and drive around in big Cadillacs. Whereas I, who worked and paid my dues, can't even buy enough food to feed myself for a week.

Nicole: ...

Daniel: And they keep coming over the border and taking our jobs. Do you know they cost us billions of dollars a year?

Nicole: Ok. I can definitely see you're upset. Who are the "they" you are talking about?

Daniel: The Blacks! And the Mexicans! They're just living off the government driving those big cars, but we struggle.

Nicole: Daniel, that's a mighty broad-brush stroke you're using there. Are you saying all Black people are living easy off the government? I'm Black, is that what you believe about me?

Daniel: No, you're different. You have a job. You're a good person. But the rest of them do. And I'm the one suffering for it. I'm not racist either. I marched with Martin Luther King. I supported civil rights for Blacks. But now, everything is affirmative action and free giveaways at the expense of White people. I mean hell! You turn on the TV and they're just shoving it down our throats. Showing Black and White families, and gay dads on TV. This is not the country I remember! I don't even see myself anymore.

Nicole: It sounds like you have been influenced greatly by what's on TV and it's upsetting to you. Are you sure that's the best source? Do you really believe the accuracy of the reports?

Daniel: Yes! Because I'm living it. This is not on the TV. They are trying to brainwash us. It's reverse discrimination and I'm mad as hell!

Nicole: I see. I thinking I'm beginning to understand. Your noticing you, or White people in general, are less and less represented compared to years past. And, this is threatening to you. You have a sense of it being unfair.

> **Reflection Point**
>
> What are your reactions to Daniel's viewpoints? What are your reactions to Nicole? Which exchanges represented race talk? What affect might have been present for Daniel and Nicole? What, if any, influences of perceived racial identity/traits might Daniel have been projecting onto Nicole? What, if any, racial identity traits might Nicole have been projecting onto Daniel?

The exchange between Nicole and Daniel exemplifies how race talk may come up in therapy. Daniel's characterization of Black people was directly challenged by Nicole, perhaps in a less than effective way. It could be assumed that Nicole experienced some angst, which may have led to taking a defensive position. Using cultural humility as a framework, Nicole, in this moment, could have internally acknowledged her own emotional reaction, which may help her maintain an other-oriented position of openness. The culturally humble position may have allowed Nicole to remain grounded in her understanding of herself as a Black woman and not personalize Daniel's characterization of Black people. Near the end of the exchange, Nicole appears to be making such a shift in acknowledging Daniel's world view and the associated distress.

Focus on the Immediate, Local, and Personal

Dialogs about race often turn to arguments that are disconnected to oneself. When this happens, race talk devolves into competitions on oppression, with participants defending, often passionately, their own position. To decrease the likelihood of monologs on one's value-based perspectives, help your clients find themselves in the discussion. In other words, make the conversation personal, about the client. To do so you may ask questions to evoke reflection on past and current experiences of race and community, as well as hopes for the future. Hope in the Cities (n.d.) created a community dialog guide that outlines questions that allow for reflection and discussion to engage in honest conversation, increase personal responsibility, and enact change. We believe this guide can be particularly helpful in using racial dialog to increase healing, resilience, and empowerment. Questions to help people reflect on themselves and the influences of their context include (Hope in the Cities, n.d.):

- When did you first realize you were a race? What happened? What did you learn about yourself? What did you learn about others?
- What kinds of neighborhoods did your grandparents and parents live in? Were they racially or ethnically mixed? What is your family's racial and/or ethnic heritage?
- How did your grandparents and parents feel about people from other racial or ethnic backgrounds? How was that communicated to you? How did that influence you?
- Describe your current neighborhood and community. Is it racially or ethnically diverse?
- What are the attitudes of your peers toward people from other racial and/or ethnic backgrounds?
- Describe one negative experience that you have had with people from other racial and/or ethnic groups.
- Describe one positive experience that you have had with people from other racial and/or ethnic groups.
- What role, if any, did race play in your choices in education for your children, housing, social club, and/or place of worship?
- Is there some aspect of your personal or group history or current reality that you feel is not being heard or acknowledged?

- Have you or any member of your family suffered or benefited from Affirmative Action? Have you or any member of your family suffered or benefitted from discrimination? Have you or any member suffered or benefited from privilege?

Creating space to discuss personal experiences may also allow reflection on one's local and immediate community. Building a sense of connection and developing ways to repair ruptures or disconnect with community can be part of the therapeutic work. Suggested questions to facilitate this level of discussion include (Hope in the Cities, n.d.):

- What political, economic, social, or cultural structures strengthen or perpetuate racial separation and injustice in your municipal area? In what way do you benefit or suffer from the status quo?
- If the people of this municipal area were able to achieve genuine racial reconciliation, what would your municipal area be like? How would it be different from your current reality?

Lastly, developing empowerment in one's immediate context is a salient feature in addressing race-based stress. Questions to increase commitment to valued actions include (Hope in the Cities, n.d.):

- In what ways do you think the American experiment of uniting diverse peoples into one great nation is incomplete? Do you think that not enough, enough, or too much has been done to redress past injustices? What are the reasons for your conclusion?
- What is forgiveness? What is repentance? Are either or both an important part of the racial reconciliation process?
- It has been said that, in a broken relationship, it is often the injured party who has to take the first step towards reconciliation. What in your personal experience leads you to believe this is true or not true? Why or why not?
- What specific steps or actions would be needed to move toward your vision of genuine racial reconciliation? What are the

obstacles to building this vision? Identify the groups/individuals who are already building positively with whom we might partner.

Focusing on the personal, local, and immediate will help your client identify their fears and angst about race talk. It is also helpful in identifying the harmful impact of race-based stress while building a way forward through empowerment.

Address the Topic of Race as Potentially Relevant to Therapeutic Issues and Discussion

Not every Black client will be interested or in need of addressing negative racial encounters. Providers can use their clinical judgment to make this determination in collaboration with their client. However, you are able to provide feedback for consideration about potential connections between race-based stress and other clinical concerns disclosed by your client. Take for example the exchange between Mauve, a 30-year old Black female client, and her therapist. Mauve is presenting for a therapy intake due to increasing irritability and angst following her recent move to a predominantly White city:

> Mauve: I'm just not myself. I have a short temper and just snap at people. I don't know why I'm doing this.
>
> Therapist: I can see this behavior is very troublesome to you. Share with me the most recent time you noticed snapping at people.
>
> Mauve: Well, I just started this job at a call center. We are in orientation and it's just the people there, I get so bothered. Like the other day, we were working on our computers on a particular exercise, the trainer called me over to her work station to give more guidance. I didn't think to lock my computer. I know we were told to do that before we leave our work area, but we were only in training. Anyway, when I get back to my work station, the information on my desktop is upside down. Someone changed my setting while I was with the trainer, I didn't know how to change

it back and was so irritated because there were snickers around me. Its like I'm being singled out.

Therapist: I can see how you would be upset with someone rearranging your stuff. I am wondering, though, what else has happened that you feel singled out?

Mauve: Well ... everyone seems younger than me ... and I don't know. I don't really associate with them or anything, like on breaks. Oh! And that's another thing that's not like me. I use to be sociable and outgoing. I just don't know what's wrong with me.

Therapist: I see, I see. Let me just recap a bit of what I'm understanding from what you've shared so far. You've recently moved to the city with your husband and two young children because he was stationed out here, you're not really connected to a community yet, and you've started a job where you don't feel you fit in and are experiencing some othering behavior from your peers. It is no wonder you are having a hard time! And yet, there is another part I am wondering about, are there any others that look like you in any of these new spaces?

Mauve: [slight pause] ... well, no, not really. I mean there is one other girl at work that isn't White, but I think she's Hispanic. I'm the only Black person in my training group. And, I haven't yet seen any other regular co-workers yet. I hope there are other Black people working there.

Therapist: Ok. Do you think that being an "only" Black person in these spaces contributes to some of your current distress?

Mauve: ... uh ... I hadn't really considered it, but I think it does ...

Therapist: How so?

The above exchange can then lead to further assessment of race-based stress and the development of a treatment plan to address all of Mauve's presenting concerns. Notice the therapist asked questions to elicit and broach the role and/or impact of race on Mauve's current experiences. When using methods like eliciting and broach, you are *not* coming from a place of questioning, but opening up the dialog in such a way that the client can explore their experience in a supported fashion. The BELIEF method is a particularly useful tool for eliciting exploration. This method allows you to join the client in conceptualization of the problem, check for your accurate understanding, validation of experiences, and normalization of impact on the client's life. The elements of the BELIEF model are highlighted below.

Belief: What caused the problem?
- You're looking for what occurred from the client's perspective. Avoid automatically looking for alternative explanations.

Explanation: Why did it happen?
- How are your clients making sense of the experience? Ask follow-up questions to elucidate the story the client has constructed around the problem.

Learn: Help me understand.
- Check-in to make sure you are accurately tracking the client's experience. In certain contexts, it's okay to ask for further clarifications on topics that are foreign to you with the intent of better understanding the person's experience. However, this should not divert away from the client exploring their racial trauma/distress.

Impact: What is the impact on your life?
- Allow space for your client to reflect on the impact of the injury sustained by the problem. Integrating the concept of injury in the problem emphasizes the nonpathological process initiated by an act that damages or hurts and the resulting reactions that can impair your client's functioning. This will also allow you to better assess and identify reactions that integrate the situational (external) and dispositional (internal) elements in the context of an individual's life history and experiences.

Empathy: "Must be very difficult."
- Empathy is an act of joining with your client where they are and sitting in the experience with them.

Feelings: How are you feeling about it?
- Engaging with your clients in this way allow you to take an open and curious stance about other's cultural beliefs and values rather than presumptuous about how to make it better.

To illustrate the application of the BELIEF model, we present the case of Winston, a 22-year-old Black male. Winston is seeking therapy to address complaints of anxiety and difficultly building friendships.

Therapist: Tell me more about what has been distressing to you. [Belief]

Winston: I don't know. I just feel on edge all the time. I feel I have to be vigilant around people because I never know what they are going to say or do. I wake up everyday and have to prepare myself to go out into the world. It's like I have to put on armor just to be safe.

Therapist: That certainly sounds exhausting. What do you think is happening or has happened that you're needing this armor? [Explain]

Winston: I don't know exactly … it's just I've been noticing a lot lately … about how people react to me as a Black man. Like I have to regulate my tone because they may get scared, but I'm just happy or excited. But if they're scared then I'm the threat and I have no power to defend myself. And if I do defend myself then I'm even more at risk. And I don't think its fair.

Therapist: As a Black man, you are having a unique experience. Just because of how you look it seems that others in your environment react to you negatively. Their reaction does not seem to be based on you, but on their perception of you. In order to manage others' reactions, you change how you behave and that still doesn't help. This causes lot of anxiety and a sense of injustice. Am I understanding this right? [Learn]

Winston: Exactly! I'm making myself smaller to appease them. And, it's not right.

Therapist: I can definitely see the injustice in this. Can you share more about the "they." Is it specific to people in your friend or work circle? [Learn]

Winston: It's everywhere. It's White people ... in my environment, at work, when I go out, when I turn on the TV. It's like I can feel their energy. Like I know they have a problem with me just being in the same space. You can just feel it. Like they expect me to be ignorant or a thug.

Therapist: This experience is wounding in many ways. How else have you noticed it impacting your life? [Impact]

Winston: I'm more angry. Even talking about it now, I'm tight. I replay situations in my head of things I wish I did or said. But when I do, I'm the bad guy or the one that has the problem. It's like I constantly have to prove myself.

Therapist: I can see and hear your distress. And, it feels to me some helplessness is there too. Like you don't have any control or say. [Empathy]

Winston: Exactly!

Therapist: If you were to name feelings that go with this experience, what would they be? [Feelings]

Winston: I feel like the world is against me. I constantly have to be on my guard.

Therapist: I hear you. You're identifying specific thoughts that come up around this experience. What would you say are the emotions that go with those feelings? [Feelings]

Winston: Anger, uneasy, stress. I feel embarrassed sometimes. And a little hopeless that anything will change.

The therapist's use of the BELIEF model accomplished several objectives: joining/rapport building, validation/normalization, and information gathering. From this point the therapist can then begin to use specific models of intervention.

> **Reflection Point**
>
> With this information from Winston, conceptualize the problem from your chosen therapy model. What would be your next response to Winston's disclosure?

Acknowledge Multiple Identities and Intersectionality of Identities

There are many ways people are culturally diverse (and experience the "-isms" and "-ics"). During racial dialogs, you may encounter *whataboutism* statements. Whataboutism is characterized as attempts to discredit an opponent's position by charging them with hypocrisy without directly refuting or disproving their argument (Wikipedia, 2019). In the context of race talk, whataboutism attempts to deflect from discussions about race and racism to other identified variables. For example, if a topic of systematic economic oppression in the Black community comes up, a White participant may respond with, "But I grew up poor too, so this is not about race." Or a White female participant can make a statement like "as a woman, I am just as oppressed as other minorities." These statements are valid in acknowledging other marginalized social variables, low socioeconomic status, and gender inequality. However, they also deflect from the discussion about race. In order to validate the valid (classism and sexism exist), and *not* validate the invalid (all marginalization is the same and experienced equally), clinicians can acknowledge all variables in the ADDRESSING model and their intersectionality. Intersectionality, as applied to an individual or group, acknowledges the interconnected nature of social constructs (race, class, and gender) that create overlapping and interdependent systems of discrimination or disadvantage. By recognizing intersectionality, practitioners can better acknowledge and ground the differences as well as increase empathy and understanding. Returning to the above example of a White male participant responding to economic oppression in Black communities with his own experience of economic oppression, a therapist may ask the participant to identify the impact of the experience(s) on his well-being and development. Subsequently, the participant can be guided to use this new understanding to appreciate the nuances of the experience of being from a marginalized racial group *and* economically oppressed community. There can then be personal reflection on similarities as well as meaningful differences. Such reflection will allow all involved to (1) increase ability to dispel stereotypes and misinformation about other groups, (2) decrease intimidation and fear of differences, (3) increase compassion for others, and (4) create greater sense of belonging and connectedness with all groups.

Be Present

Being present is a foundational skill in the therapeutic process. It incorporates other basic skills like active listening. Though a basic skill, being present bears repeating particularly in the context of cultural discomfort in engaging race talk or talking about race-based stress. As a practice, therapists let go of anything that might be a distraction (paperwork, caseload, etc.) and be intentional about the purpose of the moment. Another potential distraction is adhering to the fidelity of an evidenced-based therapy protocol (EBP) that does not readily address race or race-based stress. For example, you are in session six of Cognitive Processing Therapy (CPT) with the goal of reviewing the Challenge Questions Worksheet. However, your client wants to process a recent experience of perceived discrimination that occurred in the previous week. As your 45-minute session continues to tick by, you still need to present the worksheet. In this moment, your client and the therapeutic process might be better served by being present and responding to the moment in addressing the racial encountered experiences of the client. In doing so, the therapist may be able to draw connections between beliefs about the index trauma being addressed using CPT and the beliefs activated during the racial encounter. While this approach may drift from the fidelity of CPT, it would be in alignment of evidenced-based responsiveness in practice (Soto, Smith, Griner, Rodriguez, & Bernal, 2019).

Be Open to New Concepts and Perspectives

In practice, you may be introduced to concepts of identity that may not have existed in social or professional discourse in years past. The creators and innovators of new concepts are often members of that particular community. Given this fact, you may always have a learning opportunity from your client present itself in therapy. As best you can, be open to new concepts and expressions of identity that are different than your own experience and learning. Also remember that to be open to new perspectives does not necessitate agreement. You can maintain an accurate perception of your own cultural value/identities as well as hold an other-oriented position that involves respect, lack of superiority, and attunement (Hook, Davis, Owen, & DeBlaere, 2017). Read about Therapist Terry's experience in openness to new concepts of racial identity in Vignette 5.

Vignette 5

Terry is a seasoned therapist working in a community mental health clinic. He has been the lead in integrating culturally relevant assessment practice and treatment options, including starting a group for healing racial trauma. He leads monthly consultation group with his peer therapists regarding addressing race-based stress with clients. Terry begins individual therapy with a new client, Rick, who is a 44-year-old male. As Rick shares his experiences of mental health symptoms, including a previous diagnosis of PTSD, he also highlights how he is becoming more disgruntled at work.

Rick is employed as a logistics coordinator in a large office building. Part of his job is delivering requested materials to different departments within the company. Rick explains several instances when employees have treated him with condescension and disrespect. As Terry listens to the experiences, he begins to formulate a hypothesis about Rick's triggers and coping behaviors. Terry also begins to suspect that Rick's racial identity may also be influencing responses from his work environment. Terry introduces the concept of microaggressions to Rick using experiences he has had as a Black man. Terry states:

> As a Black man, there are many stereotypes that people will put on us without knowing anything about us. For example, we are expected to be athletes because we are both over 6' tall. Because of this stereotype, even well-meaning people will unintentionally say things that are slights.

In response, Rick stated:

> I can sort of see what you're saying, but I'm not Black, I'm Moor. Black refers to a color and I am not a color. It was a term developed by enslavers to denigrate and steal the history and intellectualism of the Moor. To be called such is a slight.

Terry, taken aback, quickly apologizes about his assumption and asks Rick to share more about how he thinks of himself as a racia-cultural being. Rick proceeds to share about the Moorish temple and practices. He even invites Terry to read one of the Moor pamphlets. After the session, Terry reflects on his negative reactions to Rick's conceptualization of Black being a negative term. Terry holds a strong sense of pride in his Black identity and felts an urge to share his perspective with Rick. Before doing so, Terry reaches out to another therapist in the clinic who is also in the consultation group. After explaining what he wishes to present to Rick at the next session, the other therapist asks Terry whose needs are going to be met if he engages in the planned discussion. Terry is then able to verbalize the insight that it would likely be his own needs and not consistent with supporting Rick's identity and using its inherent resilience to manage symptoms and environmental stressors. Terry then sets a plan to engage in weekly consultation about the work done in therapy so as to not impose his ideas on Rick.

It's OK to Disagree

There may be times you struggle with being open, especially if a new concept of identity conflicts with your own values. Avoid attacking, discounting, or judging the beliefs and views of your client. Instead, maintain your other-oriented stance and welcome disagreement as an opportunity to expand your cultural knowledge. Ask questions to understand the other person's perspective and experiential realities. Use the value conflict model presented in Chapter 2 to manage the experience and make appropriate treatment decisions with your client.

Check Out Assumptions

Adopting a cultural humility approach also means accepting that you do not have to know everything about every cultural being or group. There can be a sense of liberation with being culturally humble as it allows you to continue to learn more about yourself and others. You will not need to know the experience of race-based stress for every client. Instead, you can use tools like the BELIEF method to explore and ask questions as needed. That is not to say you will never make assumptions, but that you are intentional in identifying your assumptions and checking them.

Be Attuned to and Address Cultural Transgressions

Even with our best intentions and best culturally humble practices, we can still "blow it." According to the literature, therapists regularly perpetrate microaggressions in therapy. It is important to own our ability to have a negative impact on the client in therapy despite our best intention. When we become aware of committing a microaggression, either from our own awareness or from feedback from our clients, reacting, explaining, or defending your actions is countertherapeutic. Such responses can be triggering or retraumatizing. Instead, acknowledge the feedback received, express appreciation for their willingness to share their experience in the moment, and make a commitment to be more mindful. Read for example the interaction between a therapist and Candice, an African American mother of two young children and caregiver for her elderly mother.

> Therapist: You have incredible reserves of resilience you are drawing from to meet your family expectations. Though it is at a cost to you, you are the epitome of a strong Black woman and should take time to celebrate that!
>
> Candice: ... I'm so tired. I am tired of these expectations of being the strong Black woman. It is oppressive in and of itself! I had hoped that I could have a place here, where I didn't have to be that. But I see you are no different. When do I get to be tired and broken and weary? Why can I not stop caring about everyone and everything else but myself?! Just you saying that makes me feel less than. I ain't nobody's Aunt Jemima. And I would appreciate it if you would not put that on me!
>
> Therapist: ... When I said you are the epitome of a strong Black woman, I made an assumption about you and your values. I can see my comment was insensitive and invalidating. I am truly sorry. I did not consider the oppressive nature of being "the strong black woman." Thank you for telling me the hurtful impact of my words and limited understanding. I will endeavor not to make such assumptions again.

Reflection Point

As you read the above exchange, what reactions did you have to Candice? What reactions did you have to the therapist's response? Would it be difficult for you to respond in the same way as the therapist? Would it be easy for you to respond in the same way as the therapist?

The therapist's response to Candice is an example of a microaffirmation. Microaffirmations are small acts and gestures of inclusion and caring through active listening, recognizing, and validating experiences, and affirming emotional reactions (Rowe, 2008). In this therapeutic context, the therapist's microaffirmation was an intentional communication that validated Candice's experiential reality, expressed value for her as a person, and offered commitment to act as an ally. Microinterventions are also a method to counteract microaggressions in therapy. Microinterventions disarm microaggressions by (1) making racial experiential realities visible in treatment, (2) offering specific behaviors the therapist can engage in to address microaggressions when they arise, and (3) removing barriers to therapeutic engagement/process that may otherwise be perpetuated (Sue et al., 2019). An effective use of a microintervention can be observed in the exchange between Candice and the therapist. Specifically, when the therapist states, "When I said you are the epitome of a strong Black woman, I made an assumption about you and your values," she or he owned the transgression by describing what was happening, acknowledged the impact, and explicitly stated his or her intention to remove that barrier from the therapeutic work.

Summary

To be effective in addressing and treating race-based stress, having a shared language about race, racism, Whiteness, and White privilege is necessary. You will often need to co-create this language with your clients in order to promote healing and health. To do so, reflection on your own racial identity, biases, and privileges is the starting point to respond to and facilitate meaningful race talk. Such self-awareness disrupts social and academic norms that contribute to resistance, defensiveness, and hypervigilance that impede the provision of multiculturally competent care. Also, with accurate reflection of self, you will be better able to recognize microaggressions and disarm them using microaffirmations and microinterventions. Appropriately using tools like the BELIEF model increases likelihood that you and your client can explore and challenge intrapersonal and external factors inherent in race-based stress.

CHAPTER 6
Culturally Responsive Interventions

Introduction

Within the context of individual therapy, it is important to bring with you the concepts held within a multicultural orientation and engaging in race talk as discussed previously. Doing this kind of work requires bravery and flexibility on the part of both you and the client. The ability to capitalize on cultural opportunities and provide the safe space for processing while engendering hope through the implementation of skills is a delicate balance. Later we will provide a session-by-session group model for managing RBS, but in individual therapy at best it is semi-structured. At times, cultural exploration or race-based stress (RBS) will be one of the presenting issues, but depending on your setting this is unlikely. If you are in a private practice or setting that specifically markets to marginalized groups and promotes race work then often this will be discussed during the request for services or in the intake paperwork. However, in most settings it arises as a secondary issue and the onus is on the clinician to assess for these variables sooner rather than later. This will allow you and the client the space to interweave processing and skill building throughout the treatment plan. It can mean implementing interventions as they arise or, if the client lacks coping strategies in several areas, making this a focus of treatment. The goal in this section is to take interventions that you may already know and apply them in a novel way. Dialectical Behavior Therapy (DBT) has been widely researched and is effective for a wide variety of diagnoses and symptom constellations (e.g. depression, PTSD, irritability, general emotion dysregulation) and client populations in the US and around the world (Linden, 2013; DBT Research Updates, n.d.). The following interventions are not a replacement for formal DBT training. We strongly encourage you to engage in formal training in this model as it will aid in more effectively teaching and utilizing the skills in the context of RBS. Throughout this section, you will be introduced to Coretta and ways in these concepts and skills were helpful to her.

> **Reflection Point**
>
> Coretta is a 39-year-old Black female. She is originally from Ohio, but has been living in Georgia for the past three years. She is single and lives alone. She recently obtained associates degree in Business Management and works in food services. She is hoping to get promoted to a management position in the near future. She presented to therapy with symptoms of depression (i.e. low mood, sleep disturbance, low energy, irritability, and feelings of worthlessness and hopelessness). After a few sessions with her therapist, it also comes to light that she is having several stress reactions related to microaggressions at work and in her daily life. These environmental events are exacerbating her symptoms of depression. Coretta has expressed interest in reducing depression, coping more effectively with race-based stress, and figuring out how to move forward in her career.

Techniques for Individual Therapy Interventions

To begin it is important to introduce the concept of the three states of mind. It relates to the mindfulness skills within DBT, but is also a helpful standalone notion for the client. Within the framework of race-based stress, it is helpful to discuss the three states of mind and how they impact the individual acting in the best interest of themselves and the environment in which they live.

Emotion Mind

Emotion Mind refers to the part of the person that is devoid of reason. All actions are based on mood and the person may be temperamental. Emotion mind has the ability to make one feel as though they are being rational and acting in a way that is sound. The problem with pure emotion is that it is self-serving and can motivate a person to engage in extreme behaviors. This is problematic because it can often lead to unintended consequences. For instance, Coretta had an issue with her Supervisor in which she overhead him saying to a co-worker that he "would never date a black woman because they are loud and aggressive." These words were understandably hurtful and angering for her to hear. Her initial emotion minded reaction was to walk over to them, say something hurtful in return, and quit. Coretta is currently living paycheck-to-paycheck and has little savings as she is paying off student loans. If she were to act on her emotion mind in this scenario it could lead to increased financial stress for her. She would be at risk of losing her housing, losing her insurance, and not being able to continue in therapy.

Logic Mind

Logic Mind is the part of the person that is devoid of emotion. It is governed by facts, reason, and practicality. Someone in logic mind will not consult their feelings or those of others or think about values or moral codes. The problem with pure logic is that it doesn't pay attention to humanity. An essential aspect of being human is our emotions. What enjoyment can a person have if they don't have emotions? For those coming from marginalized groups, they often feel dejected and ostracized in their daily lives and finding healthy ways to connect and relate to themselves and others is a primary goal of treatment. Logic mind gets in the way of this premise. An example of Logic Mind for Coretta in this scenario is her ignoring her emotional experience and being task focused solely on obtaining her promotion. One way this could play out is her being ingratiating toward her supervisor and putting herself in a position to be the butt of his jokes.

Wise Mind

Wise Mind is the bridge or middle path between emotion and logic mind. Wise mind allows the person to take their emotional experience into account and reflect on how to best proceed in a way that honors the individual and natural limitations of the outside world. For instance, with Coretta this may mean coming to her therapy session and engaging in pro/cons and problem solving (discussed later) to determine the best course of action in this situation. She can explore the risks and rewards of staying in this job or finding another one. She can also cope ahead (discussed later) and plan out how to be skillful based on her choices. It is imperative to help a client develop their wise mind as it will allow them to build a worthwhile existence despite the existence of racism, sexism, homophobia, etc.

Mindfulness

On paper, mindfulness is a simple skill that, at its most basic level, requires us to bring awareness to the present moment through our five senses. However, in practice it is actually quite difficult. For those coping with race-based stress and trauma, present moment awareness can painful. Trauma keeps the mind everywhere but the present. The person is either thinking about past traumas that have occurred or being hypervigilant about future trauma that can/will occur. These behaviors can compound the amount of mental, emotional, and physical toll that stressors take on the individual. As such, an active mindfulness practice is essential.

While Marsha Linehan didn't created mindfulness, the way it is displayed in her DBT skills manual (Linehan, 2015) is a good entry point for those that may be unaware of what practice entails. Also, some may be deterred from engaging in mindfulness practice if it appears ambiguous or seemingly spiritual. DBT presents six tangible skills as the basis for mindfulness and opens the door for starting the practice in ways that the client feels most comfortable. While mindfulness meditations are helpful, many clients may have difficulty in the beginning for a variety of reasons (i.e. difficulty disconnecting from thoughts, trouble breathing, judgments) and may need to experiment in other ways (e.g. body focused practice like walking or yoga or utilizing their five senses with mindful eating). DBT describes the practice of mindfulness as six fundamental skills: observe, describe, participate, nonjudgmentally, one-mindfully, and effectively. The first three are the "what" skills, that is, what you are doing when you are practicing mindfulness. The latter set are the "how" skills, which is how you go about practicing mindfulness. These are described below.

Observe

The observe skill requires the person to notice what is happening through their five senses (e.g. touch, taste, smell, hearing, vision), on purpose, in the present moment. It is also necessary to have attentional control, but to be open to the sensory experiences that come about naturally. Observing requires being mindfully aware of what is happening both within and outside of the self. The goal of the observe skills is not to hold on to or push away anything in our experience, but to acknowledge it and bring our attention back to the present moment. For example, a person may be attending to the breath and a thought may arise of a microaggression experienced at work. An unmindful approach would be engaging with this thought in such a way that it takes us away from the breath. In such a case, the person is now either departing on the "thought train" or actively trying to derail it by pushing the thought away. Instead, our goal is to let the thought pass and redirect attention back to the breath in an "I see the train, but I'm not buying a ticket" fashion. Observing also involves wordless watching, which is experiencing but not labeling the sensations and stimuli that arise. Labeling requires the describe skill.

Describe

Describing involves putting words on your observed experiences. For instance, "I am having the thought that this is unfair," describes the thought without engaging with the thought. Describing requires labeling what you observe through your senses without your interpretations, judgments, assumptions, and opinions. The goal is to be concrete, specific, and stick to the observable facts. For example,

> When I went to the fast food restaurant and paid for my food the clerk put the money on the counter instead of in my hand. I had the thought this was disrespectful. I also felt a mix of sadness and anger to what was happening to me in that moment.

Developing the ability to observe and describe nonjudgmentally sets the stage for the client to reduce their own suffering, in part through the removal of internal and external behaviors that can encourage increased or sustained negative affect (i.e. rumination or substance use) in response to the original prompting event.

Participate

In DBT, the goal of mindfulness is to fully engross yourself in the present moment, in life, nonjudgmentally. Fully participating allows us to engage with the full spectrum of life. Clients who are plagued by RBS often have trouble participating. Due to the symptomatology related to previous traumas, clients can become primed for extreme reactions or ways of being (e.g. all or nothing thinking, hypervigilance, easily startled or overwhelmed, irritability). These behaviors can lead to a skewed perspective in some cases (e.g. *all* White people are racist), an inability to experience pleasant emotions and experiences, and feeling disconnected from others. By learning how to fully participate in the present moment, your clients can reduce their own suffering and allow themselves to be connected to their experiences, the world around them, and be fully present in the lives of their loved ones.

Nonjudgmentally

Nonjudgement can be a complicated skill to get across to clients who are struggling with race-based stress. How could one not be judgmental about discrimination and oppression? Nonetheless, when a person adopts a nonjudgmental stance, it allows them to acknowledge harmful/dangerous or helpful/safe experiences. They can acknowledge their desires, wishes, values, and emotional responses to situations that arise in their lives. The goal is to not judge events or our reactions to them as "good" or "bad" and get lost in the "should." We often forget that these words are a short hand for the consequences of certain behaviors in the world. For instance, let's say you go to the grocery store and the grocer states that the cantaloupes are bad. Are they saying that the fruit needs a spanking? No. What they are communicating to you is that the food is rotten and if you eat it you may get sick. When your client comes to you and says that they are a bad person because they didn't speak up at a work meeting when a microaggression occurred, what are the consequences of that? When we judgmentally describe consequences to ourselves, it can lead to a heightened negative emotional state, which can induce feelings of helplessness. When someone feels helpless, they will typically avoid problem solving and give away more power than is necessary in a situation. For example, if a person goes about life thinking "everything is bad, it should be different, and there is nothing to be done," eventually those thoughts are going to lead to feelings of hopelessness. It is more beneficial for the person to learn to accurately state the causes and consequences of harmful experiences and how it impacts their emotional state and value systems. Once that is accomplished, a person can effectively cope with what *is* while actively working towards changing the causes and, ideally, creating better future outcomes.

One-Mindfully

One-mindfully as a skill that involves being in *this* one moment, letting go of the past and future. Often times when someone is traumatized, they carry past traumas with them and spend the present moment ruminating about future harmful events. This rumination leads to increased pain in the present moment and can begin to overwhelm the person over time. A consequence can be intense emotional outbursts that may not be congruent with the present circumstances. Additionally, rumination gets in the way of the individual fully participating in the present moment. As a result, they may miss out on connecting with others and experiencing happiness to the maximal extent.

Effectively

Effectiveness is about doing what works in a situation. It requires that the person knows what their goal or objective is and that they take the necessary steps to accomplish it. When being effective, they are being as skillful as they can be in the *actual* circumstances, regardless of whether the circumstances are ideal or not. There are a few essential elements of effectiveness, which include: (1) knowing what will and won't work in a situation, (2) being able to "play by the rules," (3) reading people and being discerning, and (4) in extreme situations, being willing to sacrifice a principle for the ultimate goal. Many clients will already have examples of them engaging in these skills. A common example could be a Black person being pulled over by the police. This can be a dangerous situation for people of color. The person may have the goal to get home safely when leaving their job. They may also have a principle of justice and fairness. When they are pulled over by the police they may feel or *know* that they were wrongly pulled over. However, they will have to be careful not to let their emotion mind get in the way of their effectiveness in this situation. They know that if they are argumentative it is more likely to lead to negative ramifications, and in the worst case scenario could lead to their death. Consequently, there are several steps that a person may take in order to get home safely, including: being polite and compliant with all requests, keep their voice low, and moving slowly. They may achieve this goal, but it comes at the expense of their principle in the moment.

Reflection Point

As the therapist, part of your responsibility is to aid the client in identifying principled actions to participate in through the accumulated positive skills discussed later. This will help reduce the emotional impact of situations in which they may have to sacrifice a principle because it is in conflict with an identified goal.

Emotion Regulation

The physical and mental effects of race-based stress are pervasive. Given the nature of the world that marginalized groups live in, it is our job to equip our clients with the skills necessary to cope with and combat the effects of oppression. To use an analogy, a good football coach must prepare their team because if they are going to play football, they are going to get hit. There are techniques that the coach can teach them to be able to take a hit with less damage and avoid hits whenever possible. However, there is no way to play the game without, at least, the risk of taking a blow each time. The goal of DBT is to build a life worth living. Consequently, opting out of the game isn't a choice and the field is teeming with adversity. Training our clients can give them the padding and the moves necessary to navigate the system as best they can with the least amount of damage and suffering. Teaching emotion regulation skills can greatly reduce suffering associated with the race-based stress and trauma that Black clients may face. The following are the recommended emotion regulation skills to use in therapy.

PLEASE Skill

Encouraging your client to properly take care of their body and mind can help to mitigate some of the effects of RBS. The PLEASE skill (e.g., Treat **P**hysical Illness, Balanced **E**ating, **A**void Mood Altering **S**ubstances, Balanced **S**leep, and **E**xercise) reminds individuals of the basic and essential ingredients of self-care that often are lacking. It especially difficult to stave off the effects of race-based stress if our emotional immune system is impacted by poor diet or lack of sleep. It is not uncommon to find clients who need help implementing a routine into their lives on a regular basis that includes these elements. Consequently, it is important to view these as necessary components and to monitor them while teaching other skills.

Improving the Emotional Immune System: PLEASE

Treat **P**hysical Illness: take care of your body. If you are feeling ill, don't delay in taking medication or seeing your doctor.

Balanced **E**ating: don't over or under eat. Limit foods that can make you more emotional (i.e. sugar, caffeine, fried foods). Instead opt for lean proteins, fruits, vegetables, complex carbohydrates, and fiber. You may want to speak to a nutritionist or dietician prior to making changes.

Avoid Mood Altering Substances: limit or eliminate alcohol and illicit substances. While marijuana may be legal in your state, be sure to fully understand the effects that it has on your body (e.g. some people report increased paranoia or irritability while using the substance). Additionally, using substances as emotional self-medication is never a good thing.

Balanced **S**leep: Most adults need seven to nine hours of sleep per night. Ensure that you set up a sleep hygiene routine that allows for sufficient rest.

Exercise: whether you are working or in school, most people have sedentary lives that are not good for their overall health. Make sure that you get some small amount of exercise daily. It is good for your cardiovascular and mental health to engage in aerobic activity. Always speak to your doctor prior to engaging in any exercise program.

Tips for Better Sleep

1. Implement a consistent sleep schedule, including weekends. Try to generally go to bed and get up at the same time each day.
2. Associate your bed only with sleep and sex. This means no hanging out in your bed on the phone, watching TV, or scrolling through social media.
3. Limit eating and drinking prior to bed time. If possible, try to stop consuming foods and liquids about two hours before bed.
4. Avoid caffeine, nicotine, alcohol, and exercise late in the day as it can affect your sleep.
5. Keep the temperature of your bedroom cool as it will make it easier to sleep.
6. Make sure your space is dark and quiet. Avoid screens (TV, phone, computer) in bed.
7. If you tend to ruminate in bed, it is helpful to set aside time to journal or pray (if appropriate for you) prior to bed.
8. If the evening news makes you anxious, don't watch it. If evening television is a part of your wind down routine, choose programming that is light.
9. Hot showers are a great way to release tension in the body and mind prior to bed.
10. Sleep meditations can help to relax the busy mind and drift into sleep.

Pros and Cons of Regulating Our Emotions

Pros and Cons is a classic skill that is effective in a variety of situations. In the context of race-based stress, we have found it most impactful when deciding the merits of acting "on" or "opposite" to an emotion. As previously discussed, in many situations the individual's emotional response is justified, but may be ineffective and lead to potentially worse outcomes for them in the short and/or long term. Validating a person's experience and helping them to make wise minded decisions based on their circumstances is necessary to reduce compounding traumas.

Pros and Cons Matrix

We want to strive to be people of action and not reaction. People of action are in control of themselves. They are aware of the impacts that their behaviors (both internally and externally) have on their state of mind and their environment. Think through the pros/cons of the situation in which you find yourself. Decide whether it is worth it to you to act on your emotion mind or if you'd like to move toward your wise mind. Regardless of what you choose, you are willing to accept the consequences with dignity.

Reasons to Stay in Emotion Mind	Reasons to Move toward Wise Mind
Reasons Against Emotion Mind	Reasons Against Wise Mind

Accumulating Positives in the Short Term and Long Term

A sense of disconnection, helplessness, and hopelessness can also grow under the strains of microaggressions, systemic racism, and vicarious trauma. The purpose of accumulating positives is to create a life that feels worthwhile despite the struggles that may be encountered. The skill of *accumulating positives* in the short term allows an individual to engage in daily pleasant events to counteract the stressors present in their lives. As the clinician, it is important to have a "penny saved, is a penny earned" mentality about these daily events. Some clients may be so overwhelmed that they believe spending 30 minutes watching a comedic TV show is pointless. One idea that is worth presenting is that of the emotional bank. Skills such as PLEASE, Accumulating Positives in the Short Term (APS), and Build Mastery (discussed below) are small daily deposits into our account that can yield high returns in the long term. That TV show deposit may be enough to keep a person from going in the red. Unfortunately, withdrawals happen on a daily basis and some are larger than can be accounted for despite the best plans. As a person continues to make these small deposits they can build up a considerable barrier between themselves and emotional bankruptcy. APS also helps to support the efforts made toward Accumulating Positives in the Long Term (APL). The goal of APL is to build a worthwhile life based on one's values. Typically, APL requires multiple steps and time. The chain of events for APL is to identify the value, set goals associated with those values, and then break down the steps to accomplish each goal. For instance, in Coretta's case, financial stability is one of her values. She has already worked towards that goal by going back to school and completing a degree. However, it took her two years to complete her degree so the main payoff was delayed for two years. She was not engaging in APS on a regular basis and she verbalized an increase in depressive symptoms and stress during that time period. Consequently, she is proud of herself for persevering and getting her degree, but is unable to feel the full positive effects of her efforts due to feeling "worn out."

Identifying Pleasant Events

Pleasant events can be internal (thoughts, affirmations, memories) or external (going for a walk, working on your car). Below, please make a list of pleasant events that you can participate in the present moment. These should include solo activities or ones that involve others. Other things to consider are ease of access. For instance, if weather or amount of energy is a factor, have a mix of indoor versus outdoor activities. If money is a factor, make sure to include free or low-cost activities Set an intention for a minimum of one internal or external pleasant event each day.

Steps to Accumulating Positives in the Short Term

1. Do *at least* one pleasant thing daily! Make it a priority and don't avoid or minimize the importance.
2. Avoid multitasking and utilize the one mindfully skill when participating in the identified action or activity.
3. Fully participate and engage. Focus attention on the positive, using the observe and describe skills.
4. Let go of worries about the past and future. Do not undermine the significance of this one moment by putting it on scale of all your past pains or future failings.

Use the daily scheduler to identify and accumulate positives in the short term.

Day of Week	Internal Event(s)	External Event(s)	Mindfully Engaged? (0–5)	Level of Pleasure (0–100)
Sunday				
Monday				
Tuesday				
Wednesday				
Thursday				
Friday				
Saturday				

Steps to Accumulating Positives in the Long Term

While accumulating positives in the short term, you will simultaneously work on long-term goals that align with your values.

Steps to APL:
1. Identify and define values that are important to you.
2. Identify and set goals that are associated with these values.
3. Choose one value and associated goals to work on now.
4. Select the goal that you feel capable of accomplishing at this time.
5. Identify the steps that are necessary to meet that goal.
6. Take one action step now. Don't avoid!

We live in a world that tries to define and place limitations on us based on our race, gender, sexuality, etc. By fully defining who you are and what are important tenets to uphold, you can create armor against the trappings of a life defined by societal standards. Spend time thinking through what your values are and what they mean to you. Be as specific as possible, the more defined the value, the easier it will be to identify steps that need to be taken. Keep in mind that you can always come back and add to, remove, or amend any part of your values and goals.

Use the planner to identify and accumulate positives in the long term.

Value	*Goals*

Returning to Coretta, here is how she filled out her APL planner.

Value	Goals
My family and friends	1. Spending time with people who are important to me 2. Trying to repair relationships that have been damaged or lost
Being financially secure	1. Try to get more hours at work 2. Get a promotion and raise at work 3. Look for a new job if necessary
God	1. Read my bible on a regular basis 2. Attend church on a regular basis 3. Try to act as a Godly person. For example, the golden rule
Being a person who knows who I am and not putting up with people mistreating me	1. Start journaling and engaging in daily reflection 2. Use the positive self-talk and affirmations that I learned in therapy to help with my self-esteem 3. Learn better communication skills so I can stand up for myself in hurtful situations in a way that is appropriate and doesn't have as many negative consequences for me

Build Mastery

Build mastery (BM) involves engaging in tasks that will lead to a sense of accomplishment. Typically these tasks are challenging yet doable. When clients are able to achieve goals, it has a positive impact on their self-esteem and feeling competent and capable as a person. This may counteract some of the feelings of helplessness and hopelessness that can be generated in the face of RBS. In teaching this skill and differentiating it from APS/APL, it is important to highlight the outcome of pleasure versus productivity or accomplishment. When engaging in APS, my goal is engage in a way that induces pleasure in the present moment. BM may or may not be pleasurable. For instance, the client may set a goal to clean their kitchen and will have a sense of accomplishment when they complete this task. A sense of achievement is a positive feeling for people. However, the act of sweeping the floor or washing the dishes in and of itself may not be pleasurable. Furthermore, when engaging in APL, it may require the use of BM to complete the steps necessary or it could be used on its own. For example, Coretta has a value of "being a person who knows who I am and not putting up with people mistreating me." One of the goals she set was to journal on a daily basis. Coretta finds this difficult because she has trouble finding the time to journal and is critical of inner experiences and writing ability. Despite these challenges, she recognizes that inner reflection is a strategy she can use to deepen her awareness of herself and the world around her. Additionally, she views it as a strategy for self-soothing that could be helpful. One way to use BM is to create the appropriate amount of strain in the situation. Journaling daily as a first step will likely lead to failure and increase her self-doubts. In her therapy, she decided to start with two days per week and scheduled time to engage in writing for at least ten minutes. Once she is doing this with relative ease, she gradually increases her days until the goal is met. Another way in which BM was beneficial is that it increased her overall confidence in her writing ability. Due to this increased confidence, Coretta began to write letters to politicians as a way to engage in advocacy.

The skill of build mastery is complimentary to accumulating positives in that it helps to foster a sense of capability and accomplishment, which can lead to a sense of empowerment. Feeling capable and productive can reduce feeling overwhelmed and out of control. Consequently, it is important to challenge ourselves in small ways on a regular basis. Such challenges can be as simple as crossing something off your task list (e.g. doing laundry) or an activity that has multiple steps over time (e.g. learning a language). The important thing is to pick something difficult but ultimately possible to achieve. For instance, don't set a goal to run a 5k today when you've never run more than 20 yards in your entire life. Instead, you may want to break that goal into multiple steps and follow a staged program like "Couch to 5k." Additionally, you want to continue to challenge yourself overtime, so gradually increase the intensity of the activity chosen (e.g. if you are running 1k easily, you may want to increase to 1.5k). What is difficult can change day-to-day. There are times when you may feel so worn down that taking a shower may be a build mastery activity. Always remember to have compassion for yourself during these times.

Use the activity schedule to develop your build mastery skills.

Day of Week	Build Mastery Activity	Level of Difficulty: Too Easy, Just Right, Too Hard	Feelings Before	Feelings After
Sunday				
Monday				
Tuesday				
Wednesday				
Thursday				
Friday				
Saturday				

Fact Checking, Opposite Action, and Problem Solving

The following three skills can be used in combination or separately when teaching ways to regulate daily emotional experiences associated with race-based stress.

Fact Checking

Fact checking involves looking within to make sure that the emotional or behavioral reaction is concordant with the event itself. Repeated stress may cause an individual to be hypersensitive to trauma-associated stimuli. Consequently, their emotions and actions may be in response to their interpretation of events and not necessarily the event itself. Additionally, due to hypersensitivity to certain stimuli they may be primed for an intense emotional reaction which can lead to other unwanted emotions (e.g. guilt) or consequences. Checking the facts allows the individual the opportunity to take control of their responses and determine a plan of action. It can be the precursor to opposite action and problem solving (discussed below). When discussing fact checking, the question is whether the emotion is justified or not. "Justified" is determined by being supported by the observable facts of the circumstance. Most situations that arise for people from marginalized groups are nuanced. Therefore, the skill must be taught and utilized artfully to avoid invalidation. When teaching this skill, we often focus on letting the client know that it is about ensuring that information isn't missing or being considered through our trauma lens (emotion mind) instead of our warrior lens (wise mind). A warrior is astutely aware of their internal and external experiences and can strategically navigate those spaces with the highest probability of obtaining the desired outcome.

Opposite Action

If it is determined that the (1) emotion, (2) the intensity of the emotion, or (3) the duration of the emotion doesn't fit the facts, then the individual is guided to engage in opposite action. Furthermore, even if the elements do fit the facts, but it is determined that the emotion is ineffective and causing harm, the client will still want to use opposite action to reduce their own suffering. The idea behind opposite action is that emotions have associated action urges. When a person acts on these urges, it increases or sustains the emotion. For instance, let's think about a client who is experiencing depression. Their action urge is to isolate and this is expressed by them not answering calls from friends and lying in bed all day while engaging in negative self-talk. If acted upon, these action urges will allow the emotion to persist. If depression is unwanted, then the person could refrain from acting on the action urge and identify counter actions to reduce the emotion. In this circumstance, the person might want to engage by spending time with a friend to generate pleasant affective experiences. Overtime, a person can become more resilient to intense emotional experiences through a combination of emotional regulation skills like opposite action and distress tolerance.

Problem Solving

After engaging in fact checking and opposite action, the next step is to engage in problem solving, if it is determined that the situation is problematic. Many people in chronically stressful situations can develop a sense of helplessness. Problem solving can help the person feel more empowered. For example, cultural mistrust or paranoia is normal within the Black community due to a long history of systemic racism. For members of the Black community, there may be many instances in which a fear or anxiety reaction is justified. However, living in a constant state of fear has significant consequences for the individual. There are several ways to engage in problem solving around justifiable fear such as removing or avoiding the threat, or engaging in activities that allow for greater sense of control (e.g. build mastery). While it may seem impossible to remove racism from one's daily life, there are several things that can be done to improve the overall environment. For example, clients can work to create an environment with likeminded and supportive people. They can take breaks from consuming content that is triggering (e.g. political news and social media). Additionally, the client may choose to engage in building mastery through a combination of goals (e.g. learning a second language and seeking out opportunities for community action).

Steps to Fact Checking

1. What is the emotion I am experiencing? When speaking to my wise mind, does it make sense to change (reduce the intensity or eliminate) this emotion?
2. What is the event that brought about this emotion?
    a. Make sure to use observing, describing, and nonjudgmental skills when describing the facts of the situation to get a clearer picture. This includes acknowledging your own valid emotional responses to the event.

3. What assumptions or interpretations am I making about the event? Are there other ways to view the situation?
4. What is the threat for me? What is the likelihood that this threat will occur? What are other possible outcomes?
5. If this threat occurs, are there ways I can use my skills to get through it?
6. Does my emotion itself, the intensity, or the duration fit the actual facts of the situation?
   a. From my wise mind, if the answer is yes, look into possible ways to problem solve the situation.
   b. From my wise mind if the answer is no, look to opposite action.
7. If the answer to question 6 is yes, ask yourself "Even though it fits the facts, is it harmful to me to keep this emotion around in its present state (e.g. will I suffer more, will it cause me to want to engage in actions that may lead to negative consequences)?" If so, you will still want to work on changing the emotion.
   a. These situations often require a combination of opposite action and problem solving.

Opposite Actions Tables

Emotion	Action Urge	Acting Opposite
Fear/Anxiety	Avoid	Approach the situation or person skillfully
Anger	Attack	Be respectful, and if possible, gently avoid the person or situation
Sadness	Withdraw	Engage
Guilt	Apologize, Stop Behavior	If you have not acted in a way that violates your moral code, then avoid apologizing and continue the behavior
Shame	Hide	Open up in safe spaces

Coretta's opposite actions table looks like this.

Emotion	Action Urge	Acting Opposite
Indignation (anger word)	Quit my job	Limit my time with my boss and those co-workers by only talking about work related matters. Use polite language when I am speaking to them
Disappointed and lonely (sadness words)	Go home, sleep, don't talk to anyone	Talk to my friends about it, talk to my church community, do things that are fun

_____
_____
_____

Below please fill out this table with your specific emotions, action urges, and ways to engage in opposite action.

Emotion	Action Urge	Acting Opposite

Steps to Problem Solving

1. What is the problem that you are trying to solve?
2. What is the outcome that you would like to see? Remember to focus on goals that are achievable.
3. Write a list of *any* and *all* solutions that come to mind. Brainstorming is about generating ideas.
4. Choose one or two solutions that are most likely to work from the list above.
5. Put the solution(s) into action
6. If they work, keep doing them! If not, go back to your list and choose other solutions or generate new ones to try.

Coping Ahead

Learning how to cope ahead is valuable for navigating the difficult spaces that many clients have to travel within. The ability to cope ahead can allow them to feel empowered in both the present moment and the future situations that may cause them distress. You will find that most clients have both general and specific situations for which they will need a cope ahead plan (CAP). General situations are those encounters that they have had in the past that they are sensitive to and may occur again in the future (e.g. dealing with the police). Specific situations are those that are currently present (e.g. having to work closely with a co-worker who engages in microaggressions).

Cope Ahead Plan (CAP)

Describe the situation:

Describe internal emotions or reactions that may occur:

Make a game plan for the situations. Describe in detail the skills you will use to cope with the situations both externally in the environment (E) and your own internal reactions (I).

Problem E/I	Skill(s)

Imagine the situation happening while fully using your skills. Did any unexpected problems arise? If so, add them to your CAP. If not, rehearse until you feel comfortable. In this context, comfortable is defined as knowing how you will proceed and not necessarily being comfortable with what is about to happen. If the imagery is distressing, practice relaxation techniques to bring down arousal.

Distress Tolerance

Distress tolerance skills are sometimes referred to as "crisis survival skills," and are used in critical moments when the person is faced with heightened, short-term situations that threaten to overwhelm them. The following are distress tolerance skills that are useful in managing race-based stress reactions.

STOP Skill

Traumatized people often struggle with intense emotions including irritability and anger outbursts. The *STOP* skill can help to reduce environmental effects by inhibiting emotion minded reactions and creating the space for wise minded responses.

> **STOP Skill**
>
> **Stop:** freeze! Don't move! Don't speak! Your emotions are trying to get you to do something without thinking!
>
> **Take a step back:** let's take a mental and physical deep breath. Allow your mind to slow down and your emotions to cool off. Stepping away can be within your own mind or in your actual environment. Your emotions will encourage you to act impulsively, don't listen!
>
> **Observe:** use your mindfulness observe skills. What are you feeling? What are you thinking? What is happening? What is actually being said? Please observe as best you can without judgment.
>
> **Proceed Mindfully:** ask your wise mind: what can I do that will actually make this situation better instead of worse? Remember that emotion mind is an instigator! You are looking for a balanced approach so consider all the variables and proceed accordingly.

TIP Skill

Often, clients may disclose times in which they experienced intense and overwhelming emotional responses to stressors in their environment. These events may push a client rapidly and deeply into their emotion mind. In so doing, emotion minded clients may act in ways that have unintended and worsening consequences for them. The *TIP skill* is designed for those moments in which emotional arousal needs to be brought down quickly.

TIP Skill

Temperature: turn down the temperature by putting cold water on your face. The most immersive way to engage in this is by filling the sink or a large bowl with cold water. Some people like to add a few ice cubes so it is extra cold, but it is important to keep the temperature around 50 degrees Fahrenheit, or more. Other ways to use this skill include using an ice pack, or cooling towels pressed on the face.

Intense Exercise: when overwhelmed, many people feel physically agitated and "like I want to punch something." Intense exercise can help by using up that pent up energy in a way that is effective. It is important to keep in mind your physical limitations when engaging in this skill so as not to get hurt (e.g. don't try to run up several flights of stairs if you have a bad knee. Consult with your physician for safe ways to expend this energy). You want to focus on activity that gets your heart rate up even if it is only for a brief amount of time. This can be nearly anything: brisk walk, jog, run, jumping jacks, or pushups.

Paced Breathing and Paired Muscle Relaxation: when doing paced breathing, you want to breathe deeply into your belly. An easy way to see if you are doing belly breathing is to place your hands around your belly button. You should feel a slight rise and fall in that area. This is an indicator that you are expanding your lungs properly. Slow your pace of inhaling and exhaling, and make sure the duration of exhalation is longer than inhalation. A common pacing method is breathing in for five seconds, and out for seven seconds. You can shorten or extend durations based on your lung capacity.

You can add in muscle relaxation techniques with your paced breathing. One at a time, tense and relax each muscle group going from head to toe. Notice the differences in each muscle group as they go from a state of tension to complete relaxation.

Distracting

Distracting is helpful to clients when their emotional pain is intense and threatens to overwhelm them. Distraction skills are particularly useful in public situations like school, work, and recreational activities. These skills are also needed when there is a problem to be solved, but it can't be fixed immediately. It is important to remind clients that distraction is different from avoidance. Avoidance implies that the person has no intention of returning to the problem at hand. Distraction is a time-limited skill in which attention is diverted to other stimuli. There can be feelings of guilt if a client has a need to take a break from a race-based stress. They may believe they are required to be astutely aware of every overt and covert form of oppression at all times either as a safety precaution or in solidarity with their fellow marginalized people. Such thoughts and feelings will quickly lead to burn out for the person. Coping with microaggression and other forms of RBS is a marathon and not a sprint. Distracting skills, as well as the self-soothing and improving the moment skills (see below), facilitate the individual surviving the acute crisis moments that may arise throughout the course of living as a Black person. We use the acronym EMPOWER to highlight the elements of distraction we find to be useful.

> **EMPOWERment through Distraction**
>
> Enforce Limits: know *your* limits and adhere to them in a nonjudgmental fashion. Remind yourself that is acceptable to take a break and that you are not abandoning the situation or others. Set a time limit that seems reasonable to you to use distraction (this can range from five minutes to days depending on the scenario).
>
> Mental Barrier: create a mental barrier between yourself and the distressing event. This can be done internally and externally. Internal barriers involve mentally pushing

away from the stressful event. You can build an imaginary wall inside your mind between yourself and it, imagine putting it in a time-out, or setting a mental timer before you are allowed to attend to stressful images or thoughts. External ways of creating a mental barrier include a social media/news blackout or temporarily muting or avoiding individuals that increase stress.

Purposeful Participation: give back to others in small and meaningful ways. This can be volunteering, helping a friend or family member, retweeting an important cause, or giving someone a hug.

Other Emotions and Thoughts: do things that replace your negative thoughts and emotions with neutral or opposite ones. This can include watching emotional or comedic TV shows, reading a book, looking through old letters, playing games on your phone, or singing a song in your head.

Wider Focus: when we are triggered, the tendency to ruminate creates an extremely narrow focus and intensifies the pain we are feeling. Having a wider focus involves healthy comparisons which can allow us to see the bigger picture. Comparing your situation to a time when you actually felt worse and remembering that it became better over time, thinking about others that may be less fortunate than yourself, or thinking about others who are in similar situations and are coping the same ("I am not alone"), worse ("I am not as bad as I sometimes think"), or better ("by being skillful, I can improve how well I cope overtime").

Engage in Activities: do things that allow you to forget for the time being. This can be enjoyable activities like spending time with a friend or going to the movies. It can also be more neutral activities like doing laundry or going grocery shopping.

Regroup or Reset: check in with yourself to see if your overall arousal is low enough to re-engage with the situation at hand. If so, regroup and think about problem solving or other skills that may be useful in addressing the situation. If not, reset your distraction timer and come back to the situation later.

EMPOWERed Worksheet

Fill out the worksheet below to outline how you will EMPOWER yourself in your time of need.

1. What are your emotional and mental limits in this situation? Acknowledge them in a nonjudgmental fashion.
2. How much time seems reasonable to distract?
3. What are signs that you are ready to return to the situation? What are signs that you need more time?
4. Discuss what you did to practice the skill.

Skill and usage	Distress before/after 0–5 (0=I can't handle it, 5=I can cope)	Problems that arose to discuss with therapist
	/	
	/	
	/	
	/	
	/	

5. When ready to regroup, engage in problem solving to see what other skills can be useful. If you have difficulty doing this step alone, bring it to therapy, or discuss with a trusted friend or family member.

6. If you need to reset the time, don't despair! Life is hard enough without self-judgment.

Self-soothing

The purpose of self-soothing is to comfort and be kind to oneself in an effort to reduce stress and pain. It is easy for clients to wallow in pain and take part in behaviors that exacerbate the feelings or situation. When going through painful events, we train our clients to self-validate by saying, "You are in pain. What do you need?" and responding with self-soothing strategies. This is counter to the ignoring, wallowing, or a "be strong" attitude the client may utilize at the start of therapy. In DBT, self-soothing is done through the five senses. The client can use each sense individually or combine them to intensify the self-soothing if desired. For instance, the client could listen to soothing music and that could feel adequate. Alternatively, they could play music, burn a scented candle, and take a hot bath simultaneously.

Self-Love in an Unloving World

The world can take its toll on you with the small and large stressors that arise on a daily basis. Self-soothing is about taking care of yourself when stress and distress start to build. Think of things you can do that involve your five senses that you find to be stress relieving. Remember you can combine various senses to intensify the effect of the self-soothing (e.g. wrapping yourself in a fuzzy blanket while drinking hot tea and listening to jazz music). In regards to taste, be careful not to overindulge because that can lead to negative emotional experiences.

Sight	*Sound*
1.	1.
2.	2.
3.	3.

4.	4.
5.	5.

Touch	Smell
1.	1.
2.	2.
3.	3.
4.	4.
5.	5.

Taste (Don't overdo it!)	
1.	
2.	
3.	
4.	
5.	

What did you notice after using the self-soothe skill?

Improving the Moment

Improving the moment is needed in situations that may be more long-lasting and in which distracting and self-soothing may be ineffective on their own. The goal of improving the moment is to take a seemingly unbearable situation and engage in strategies that can make the present moment easier to tolerate. Tolerating the moment is not necessarily about liking or loving the moment, but taking a moment in time that initially appears unlivable and making at a minimum survivable.

IMPROVE the Moment

Imagery: use imagery to make things more tolerable. This can include imagining yourself on a beach or a place where you've always felt safe. You can imagine things going well in the end. You can also imagine that your pain is a piece of paper that you can crumple up and throw in the trash.

Meaning: find purpose in your pain. Looking for the silver lining. Return to your spiritual values.

Prayer: open yourself up to God, a higher power, or your wise mind. Give it to God. Ask for strength during your time of need.

Relaxing: engage in actions that you find to be relaxing. For example, drinking hot tea, taking a bath, getting a massage, etc.

One thing in the moment: focus your energy on one thing at a time in the present moment. This may mean focus all your attention on what you are doing (e.g. folding laundry), sensations in your body, or grounding yourself in the moment through various mindfulness techniques.

Vacation: give yourself a break from the distressing moment. Turn off your phone, take a one hour break from a hard task, go for a walk in the part, or cozy up in bed for a little.

Encouragment: be your own cheerleader! Let yourself know that you can make it through this rough time. Say things like, "I got this!" or "I'm doing the best I can," "I'll survive!"

Reality Acceptance Skills: Radical Acceptance, Turning the Mind, Willingness

Reality acceptance is accepting life on life's terms. It is a full recognition of the rules of the game (even if those rules are not in your favor). Fighting against reality is much like spinning tires when your car is stuck in mud. All it does is dig you in deeper.

Radical acceptance (RA) is a process of complete and total acceptance of reality as it stands. Not only is it an acknowledgment of the facts, but a willingness to fully participate in reality. In many cases, acceptance becomes the first step before helpful actions can occur. When a person is not engaging in acceptance, the implication is that the event has to be removed in order to move forward (e.g. "I wish this never happened," "This should not have happened," "Why did this ever happen to me?" "I can't be happy because this event happened"). Changing this mindset will open doors to new interventions within the therapy space. Accepting reality does not mean we condone the circumstances in which we find ourselves. For instance, a client who was sexually molested by a family member can choose to radically accept this fact. This does not mean that they are saying that it was okay that they were abused. They are simply affirming the fact that this is a part of their story. They are letting go of the never ending story of "why" and moving on to potentially healing the pain caused by these facts. The goal of the reality acceptance skills is to reduce suffering and allow the individual to move more freely through life despite the presence of pain.

Turning the mind and willingness are used in conjunction with RA. Within DBT, acceptance is seen as a choice. Depending on what one is choosing to accept, the person may have to make that choice several times. The more painful the event, the more effort it will take to accept. Accepting that the grocery store is out of your favorite ice cream is much easier than accepting that oppression occurs in the world. Turning the mind is moving the mind away from fighting reality to accepting reality. Willingness is accepting reality and choosing to respond in an effective way.

When to use radical acceptance:

1. When life has dealt the person pain, trauma, or misfortune.
2. When the person is in distress but not in crisis. This is for situations in which they are stressed, but not accepting them can only exacerbate the situation with additional painful emotions (e.g. suffering).
    a. For example, when Coretta temporarily lost a shift at work, she initially was not accepting of it. This led to additional frustration and irritability. Once, she was able to accept it, she engaged in problem solving and was able to communicate with co-workers that she was willing to pick up shifts and have an alternative plan to complete household errands.
3. When problem solving isn't working. It is important to make sure that the client has radically accepted all aspects of the issue. Otherwise, if they have not clearly evaluated the situation, they may be trying to solve the wrong problem or missing critical information.
    a. Coretta received a break-up text message from a man she'd been dating for a couple of months. She had already developed strong feelings for him and thought that the relationship was going well. In the message, he was clear that he had returned to his ex-girlfriend and there was no chance for reconciliation between them. For the next several weeks, she stalked all of his social media, dressed nicely and went to bars he frequented, and prayed that he would realize he'd made an error. Not accepting that he wasn't coming back kept her from focusing on processing her grief and moving toward finding someone who could reciprocate love.

What RA is *not*:

1. As discussed above, radical acceptance is not approval.
2. It is not compassion or love. Compassion and love is sometimes associated with acceptance, but it is not a necessary condition.

a. A person can radically accept that someone on the train called them the N-word, but they don't have to love them.
b. A person can radically accept that abuse happens, that economic disparity exists, or human rights are infringed upon on a daily basis without every liking or approving of these things in any way.
3. It is not giving up or giving in. As previously discussed, RA is often a necessary first step to engaging effective behaviors. It is not acquiescing to the circumstances in one's life that encourage feelings of helplessness. In fact, RA, much like the serenity prayer, is about accepting what can't be changed and changing what can be.

Steps to Radical Acceptance (OVERCOME)

Observe that you are fighting against reality.

Verify the facts. Remind yourself that it is what it is.

Explore the causes. Acceptance can be easier if you understand more about the situation that you are trying to accept. This is different from making excuses. For example, if you understand systemic racism (i.e. the history and current mechanism that support it in present day), it makes it easier to not get stuck in the "why" zone (e.g. why me, why this, why now, why still).

Be **R**adical! Commit to accepting reality with your whole self. Your mind, body, spirit. Ask yourself, "What would it look like if I were accepting this situation?" If you notice tension within yourself use other skills like mindfulness, progressive muscle relaxation, or prayer.

Cope Ahead. Make a cope ahead plan for situation that is likely to overwhelm and force you into emotion mind.

Opposite Action. Practice opposite action to move yourself into a willing space. This could mean creating a mantra of acceptance in your head that you repeat over and over, using open body language (i.e. half smiling), identifying the emotions getting in the way of acceptance and acting opposite, or imagining yourself accepting it and engaging in those actions.

Meditation. Mindfulness, relaxation, or spiritual/religious meditations can be helpful to clear the mind, remove tension from the body, or if so inclined, use prayer or similar meditations to free the spirit.

Embrace Life. Fully acknowledge that your life is worth living despite the fact that pain exists. Notice when you are refusing to accept reality and repeat steps as necessary. Have compassion toward yourself as you go through this difficult process. Be your own cheerleader.

Coretta: I was watching the news and they executed this Black man on death row even though they have new evidence that he may be innocent.

Therapist: I heard about that. It's really sad.

Coretta: They always out here killing us! Why is the world like this! I just want to give up! I've been depressed and I can't sleep. I am always worried about my brothers and sisters.

Therapist: Your experience is valid and it seems like this is causing you to suffer a lot. It feels like it relates to the radical acceptance skill we discussed a couple of weeks ago.

Coretta: That acceptance things is hard. Situations like this is some real BS!

Therapist: I agree. It is some real BS! That's the thing about accepting reality, we aren't saying it's not painful. We aren't saying that that the thing that happened isn't unfair or that we didn't wish it didn't occur. I'd love to wake up tomorrow and racism, sexism, homophobia, etc. had just disappeared!

Coretta: For sure.

Therapist: But what I want to do right now is honor your pain. Fighting against reality creates suffering. If you remember ...

Coretta: Yeah, suffering is optional and pain is mandatory.

Therapist: Right!

Coretta: So, if I stop being willful then I can take care of myself and I can figure this out.

Therapist: We can figure this out together. It sounds like the reality is that there is the possibility that an innocent man was executed. What emotions did this bring up for you?

Coretta: Sadness and disappointment. I want the world to be better.

Therapist: Let's break this down because it seems like we can use several different skills in this situation. What skills might help with your emotions?

Coretta: Probably self-soothe and some opposite action. I tend to not reach out when I'm feeling low. I want to make a point to keep talking through things with you and to my friends who won't make me feel worse.

Therapist: We've done mindfulness meditations in the past when you've been suffering and you responded well. How would it be to walk you through one now before we go any further?

Coretta: That sounds good.
Engage in seven minute mindfulness meditation

Therapist: How was that?

Coretta: I definitely feel more relaxed in my body. My heart was going when I first got in here.

Therapist: I'm glad that helped. I think the rest of the session would be a good time to make a self-soothe list for you to practice over the week. As we talk through your emotions we can identify ways to soothe. I also want to begin to problem solve your statement about wanting the world to be better. There is an organization called the Innocence Project that you may be interested in. Especially since you've taken up letter writing …

Communication Skills

Communication skills are not the first thing that come to mind for the clinician when they are coping with race-based stress. However, when working with marginalized groups, one must keep in mind that they may be exposed to hostile environments on a daily basis. Stereotypes have real world consequences for those with minority status. Some of the stereotypes associated with Black people relate to aggression and criminality. Individuals who hold implicit biases may be more likely to perceive these qualities in a Black person than someone else. Proper communication can greatly improve their ability to make it through these situations with improved outcomes. In some instances, being able to communicate effectively could be the difference between life and death. Furthermore, communication skills provide the client with the tools to be heard when they are so often overlooked. In DBT, the skills for communication are *DEAR MAN*, *GIVE*, and *FAST*.

DEAR MAN affords the client the ability to discuss objectives in a clear and direct manner. GIVE allows the person to get their point across in a way that can be heard, and is conducive for building or maintaining relationships. The old adage "a spoon full of sugar helps the medicine go down" works well here. FAST allows the person to get through the situation in a way that allows them to feel self-respect regardless of the outcome. The right combination of these skills contributes to an interpersonal dynamic that can create the opportunity for success without the individual sacrificing their integrity in the process.

DEAR MAN

> **D**escribe: if necessary, describe the situation. Remember to stick to the observable facts of the situation. "There are times

when we have arguments over the phone, and you hang up on me"

Express: express your thoughts and feelings about the event. Use I-statements when expressing yourself. "I feel frustrated, and disrespected when you hang up on me." Not "you're such a jerk for hanging up the phone."

Assert: assert yourself in the situation by either asking for what you want, or saying no to what you don't want. "I would like it if you would verbalize that you need to leave the conversation, and we both say bye instead of hanging up on one another."

Reinforce: reinforce or reward the individual for giving you what you want in the situation. "I think fights will resolve themselves a lot more quickly if we can learn how to fight fairly."

Mindful: stay mindful of your objective in the situation. Sometimes people will engage in tactics to distract you from your goal. It is important to be a *broken record*, and keep coming back to your main point. You also want to *ignore attacks* if the person attempts to threaten, change the subject, or any other behavior that will cloud your vision in the situation. Remember to keep your mind on the desired outcome.

Appear Confident: we may not always feel confident in interpersonal situations, but we want to at least be a good actor. Confident people make eye contact, speak clearly, have clear tone (not too loud and not whispering), and upright physical posture. In practice, you may want to record yourself to see if you have any habits that you want to work on.

Negotiate: we may have to compromise in a situation. Think about what you are willing to give up in order to get as close to your original objective as possible. Be willing to work with the person to look at possible alternative solutions, adjust your request, or say no for now with the option of returning to the situation later. You can also turn the tables in which you put the ball in their court and ask them what they think will work to resolve the situation, given your opposing viewpoints.

GIVE

> **G**entle: be gentle and respectful in the situation. Avoid attacking, threatening, judging, or physical acts of contempt (e.g. sucking teeth, rolling eyes, interrupting, or walking away).
>
> **I**nterested: act interested in what the other person has to say (even if you aren't actually interested). Listen to what they are saying, make eye contact, give nonverbal cues (like nodding or putting away your cell phone), lean in, and avoid talking over the other person.
>
> **V**alidate: show the other person that you understand where they are coming from, try to put yourself in their shoes. You can validate in both your words (e.g. "I can see that you are stressed") and actions (e.g. handing someone a tissue when they are crying).
>
> **E**asy Manner: think "you catch more flies with honey." Smile, use humor, and no attitude.

FAST

> **F**airness: be fair to yourself and others. You want to validate both your and the other person's point of view.
>
> Non-**A**pologetic: don't over apologize. Remember you are allowed to make requests, have thoughts, feelings, and opinions, respectfully disagree, and take up space. Stand tall, make eye contact, and validate your legitimacy as a human being.
>
> **S**tick to Values: remember your values and moral code, don't sacrifice these unless it is a critical situation. If you are in a desperate situation, don't judge yourself for having to concede as it is difficult living within a system that limits your chances of success.
>
> **T**ruthfulness: be truthful. Don't embellish or make up excuses.

Talking Points Handout

Each interpersonal situation needs the right mix of DEAR MAN, GIVE, and FAST in order to maximize the chance of success. Fill out this sheet to help you think through an upcoming interaction and prepare for the dialog you want to have with the person(s).

Describe the situation (facts only, no judgments or interpretations):

Express yourself:

What would you like to see happen (Assert)?

How can you reward the person for giving you what you want?

What are potential attacks or distractions that the person or situation may throw at you?

How will you respond to these attacks or distractions in the moment?

What are ways that you can appear confident and not overly passive or aggressive in the situation? If need be, practice this in front of a mirror, or record yourself and play back as practice.

If you end up having to negotiate, what are you willing to compromise on?

What ways can you GIVE in this situation?

How can you be FAST in this situation?

Eight Week Group Intervention Techniques

In a cost-sensitive fiscal climate of managed care, group therapy may be more efficient and offered more broadly to clients (Ford, Fallot, & Harris, 2009). Group therapy will allow people who have experienced race-based stress and trauma to heal from emotional difficulties as well as learn new skills to enhance overall wellness. New research is demonstrating the effectiveness of group intervention in this way. Carlson, Endlsey, Motley, Shawahin, and Williams (2018) developed and implemented an 18-week Race-Based Stress and Trauma Group for Veterans of Color. Utilizing objective measures and qualitative feedback from group participants, the group demonstrated efficacy in the reduction of emotional ability, increased ability to cope with experiences of racism, and an overall increased adaptive coping ability. Additionally, group members reported increased sense of camaraderie through the sharing of encounters and events that had remained unexpressed due to avoidance of judgment or victim blaming (Carlson et al., 2018). Although the authors call for additional research to refine group interventions and isolate mechanisms of change, the group model allowed members to learn that exposure to racial discrimination or RBS/trauma is not a personal flaw or personal failure but is a bi-product of systemic racism. The group process resulted in an emotional corrective experience that mitigated the psychological and physical health consequences of traumatic racial experiences. Building on Carlson et al.'s (2018) report, the following section outlines an eight-week group program for addressing race-based stress with Black clients.

Overview

The overarching aim of this group program is to help people who have experienced the lasting negative effects of race-based stress to learn skills to self-validate, build resilience, and commit to living an empowered, valued life. We titled the group Race-Based Stress and Resilience (RSR). The following are the central themes of this group approach.

Creating a Shared Language about Race and Racism

The protocol of silence about race and racism serves only to perpetuate its existence. It disempowers the experiencer from effectively confronting and disarming the mental health effects of race-based stress. A key strategy in empowering group members to manage their experiences of negative racial encounters is to provide psychoeducation about race and racism and allow them to form their own definition. In doing so, group members increase awareness and can develop and use skills to maintain and improve their well-being.

Desensitization and Reprocessing

Storytelling is a healing strategy for addressing race-based stress and traumas (Comas-Díaz, 2016). Because clients relive racial stress and trauma during the retelling of experiences, teaching desensitization strategies is essential to promote self-healing. Psychoeducation on the common physical and psychological responses to chronic exposure to RBS brings awareness to the connection between the mind and body, and positions the client to utilize skills to help regulate for symptom relief. Reprocessing of racial wounds and trauma follows effective desensitization. Therapists help group members to reprocess negative cognitions and to identify and name positive cognitions. This process fosters the clients' meaning-making of racial wounds by reframing the centrality of the event as a learning, empowering, and/or wisdom-enhancing experience (Comas-Díaz, 2016).

Identity Reformation

Our sense of self shapes and is shaped by interactions with our social realities. For members of the Black community, internalized racism generates psychological alienation, self-denial, assimilation, strong ambivalence, and cognitive distortions (Comas-Díaz, 2016) resulting in changes in the perceptions of self and others. The group activities are designed to facilitate a process of personal and social transformation as members reform and restore a sense of self through an empowered perspective.

Building Community

Clients give voice to their race-related stress and trauma by telling their story in a safe environment. Not only does this promote their agency and power over the stressful/traumatic incidents, it also provides space for participants to realize they are not alone in their experiences. Being heard and validated by group members reduces feelings of isolation and alienation. Group members can (1) become aware of their own feelings, thoughts, and needs, (2) practice expressing them, and (3) learn and practice ways of responding to the thoughts, feelings, and needs of others.

Building Resilience

Resilience is essential to bounce back from adversities quickly and with less stress. Awareness about how much resilience one has at any given moment is essential. Equally essential is how to rebuild resilience reserves and how to effectively use resilience. Resilience is evidenced by: (1) holding a positive view of self and confidence in one's strengths and abilities; (2) regularly make realistic plans and carrying out the plans; (3) effectively experiencing and expressing emotions; (4) skillfully communicating with others; and (5) utilizing good problem-solving skills.

Empowerment

The process of becoming stronger and more confident, especially in controlling one's life and claiming one's rights, is interconnected with resilience. In the service of empowerment, learning is capitalized when it is based on the experiential realities of the client rather than lectures from the therapist. Facilitating empowerment involves eliciting feedback from group members, encouraging creativity and curiosity, and providing exercises for self-reflection. In doing so, clients may experience collective agency and motivation for social action.

Initial Assessment

While group therapy is an efficient and effective intervention, it may not be the best fit for every client. To optimize your group, consider setting criteria to screen the appropriateness of potential members and reduce selection errors (i.e. mismatch between therapeutic modality and a client's mental health needs) (Bernard et al., 2008; Linden, 2013). The ideal participant may be functioning well overall, but experiencing mild to moderate mental health symptoms. However, you may want to set exclusion criteria for people who are experiencing uncontrolled or poorly controlled mental health symptoms (i.e. mania, suicidal or homicidal ideation, active hallucinations, etc.) until both you and the client determine the symptoms are better managed. As the group therapist, you have the responsibility to avert dangerous, threatening, or destructive behavior to other clients. An initial assessment will decrease the likelihood of engaging a client in treatment that is ineffective or countertherapeutic.

Once you have set your group criteria, it is also important to have a brief pre-screening or assessment for interest in the group to provide an overview of what the format and goals of the group are and what will be expected by the group participant. This brief assessment can be conducted over the phone or in person. The key is making sure you and your client are able to determine the merits of engaging in the group. Essential pre-group orientation questions may include:

What are your treatment goals/plan?
How do you see this group meeting them?

What might be challenging for you?

What might be rewarding for you?

Additional questions may be determined by your setting needs or facility processes. Ultimately, thoughtful pre-screening measures will likely increase group retention because your members have been oriented to the process, content, and expectations for group participation.

Lastly, the brief assessment allows you the opportunity to attain informed consent from your client. Your informed consent should include group rules, goals, and methods. Be sure to review confidentiality for group therapy, specifically highlighting the client's role in maintaining confidentiality. While a group member may not share the same legal and ethical obligations as a therapist, you will want to emphasize the expectation that all group members agree to protect the identities of fellow members and should not discuss another member's personal history with anyone else. Review your ethical and legal obligations for confidentiality and their limits when concerned about the safety of the group member or others. Clearly communicate to your potential group member what behaviors or conduct will result in discharge from the group. For example, you may emphasize the importance of group therapy being free from discrimination, sexual misconduct, or behaviors that make a member feel uncomfortable, harassed, or threatened. You may provide specific examples of such behaviors (i.e. name-calling) as well as co-create the conduct expectations with your client (and group) by eliciting feedback.

Structure

An eight-week, closed group will allow for group development across two phases of the work: Sessions 1–3, psychoeducation about race-based stress; Sessions 4–8, identity reformation, building resilience, and empowerment. The sessions build upon the previous ones and incorporate the presentation and practice of skills to enhance overall well-being. To achieve its aims, the group should have 6–12 members and be offered weekly for 75–90 mins.

Group Session Structure

1. Group Check-in/Review of Practice Assignments
2. Exercise/Activity
3. Process/Discussion
4. Practice Assignment
5. Summary

As described above, the RSR group prioritizes the expression of negative racial encounters and the development of skills for resilience and empowerment. The format of the group uses an integrated psychoeducational and psychotherapy structure. This integrated group will help group members remediate psychological problems associated with race-based stress and trauma through interpersonal processes and problem-solving, as well as focused development of group members' thinking, feeling, and behavioral skills through structured learning within and across group meetings.

Your role as the group facilitator may initially begin as teacher, providing (1) factual information (i.e. introducing the concept of race-based stress/trauma, racial identity development, defining microaggressions, etc.), (2) leading discussions about it, and (3) helping group members incorporate the information into their lives through skill-building exercises (i.e. mindfulness practices, relaxation/grounding exercises, communication skills, etc.). It is imperative that you also allow for exchanges among members of the group to provide a level of support, caring, and confrontation not always found in individual therapy.

Managing Affect in Group Race Talk

In Chapter 5, we acknowledged that engaging in race talk can engender intense emotions, particularly during the expressing of different perspectives, world views, and lived experiences. In homogeneous groups, i.e. all Black participants, there may be a unique quality to the intensity of emotions and mistrust expressed. Prior to joining the group, Black members may utilize survival mechanisms like "playing it cool" to conceal true thoughts and feelings and appear serene, calm, or nonreactive in the face of racism. This is a transgenerational coping mechanism that protects Blacks living in a highly racist society. It includes indirect rather than direct expressions of hostility, aggression, and fear (Sue, 2013). Historically and currently, Black people who engage in true expression of thoughts and feelings in response to racism may face threats to their rights, livelihood, resources, freedom, and physical safety (e.g. Sandra Bland, after directly expression her irritation during a traffic stop, was forcibly removed from her car, detained, and later died in jail). When creating a safe space, you are offering, perhaps for the first time, an opportunity for Black clients to express their experiences of racism without talking in code or having to suppress their emotions. Consequently, you may anticipate verbalization of hostility, rage, disgust, and even hate. There may also be prejudicial comments made against White people and White society as well as hostility directed toward members of the Black community who are seen as "selling out." These expressions in group may be a direct result of accumulated stress and traumas. It is imperative that you not shut down the content when such discussions start. Instead, help group members make sense of their emotions while validating them and encouraging expression of the beliefs/thoughts that are underlying, or even fueling, the emotion. In this way, you can control the process rather than the content of the dialog. You are encouraged to use your clinical judgment regarding maintaining safety of group members and others. Do not dismiss statements of thoughts to harm self or others. Utilize risk assessment processes to check-out any concerns that may arise.

Group Sessions

The following are brief descriptions of the weekly group session content and accompanying handouts. Our intent is to provide a structure for developing and implementing a Race-based

Stress and Resilience group. However, we encourage creative modification such that the group meets the needs of the community(ies) you serve.

Session 1

The thematic focus of the first session is to build community and create a shared language. After reviewing the group expectations/rules, confidentiality, and any other logistical processes (e.g., as determined by you or your organization), facilitate an invitation to be present and acknowledged in the group. You may be creative with introductions, using ice breakers or other activities. However, keep in mind that you do not want to take more than ten minutes to do so as you may not have time to complete the other activities for the session. The goal of the introductions is to encourage dialog between members and reinforce personal disclosures (i.e. hopes/goals of group participation, etc.). The main objective of the first session is to co-create understanding of the concepts of race and racial stress/distress that will then be the reference point for future discussions. This may be more academic, or lecture-style, however, it is important to empower group members to name that which has been made invisible in the larger culture. The YouTube clip will then provide a link between academic concepts and personal, lived realities. Be sure to review the video clip prior to showing it to the group to process through your own reactions. After viewing, use the presented process questions or develop other process questions that facilitate personal reflection on experiences of being "a race." Because the clip and subsequent discussion may be triggering, be sure to teach/practice a relaxation skill or mindfulness activity to help group members regulate emotional responses. This practice also aligns with the practice of desensitizing to racial stress and traumas. To end, the session, provide a summary of the topic and discussion and share brief description of the second session.

Session 1 Agenda and Activities

- Review group rules and expectation, confidentiality and privacy
- Facilitate introductions, giving first names and what members hope to get out of the group
- Understanding race, racial stress, and distress
    - View YouTube video "When I first realized I was Black"
        - Process and discussion (reactions to the clip)
        - Reflection exercise: what is a "race"? When did you first know you were a race? What have you learned about yourself as a race since then?
    - Present "Defining Race and Racial Stress" handout and discuss
- Mindfulness/relaxation exercise
- Wrap-up

WORKSHEET 6.1

Group Expectations and Agreements

The Race-based Stress and Resilience group will address the unique challenges and psychological impact that experiences of racism, discrimination, and prejudice have had on the health and psychological well-being of people of color.

The goals of this eight-week group are to:

- Promote healing and self-care
- Enhance adaptive coping and resilience
- Increase positive racial identity
- Motivate empowerment and community engagement

To receive the most from the group, we ask you bring willingness to engage in the following:

1. <u>Attendance.</u> Make an effort to show up each week. Each session builds on the other. Be on time. This demonstrates respect of other group members.
2. <u>Confidentiality.</u> Who you see and what you hear stays within the group. This provides trust and the freedom for all to be open and honest with themselves and others.
3. <u>Cell phones.</u> Please turn them off or place on silent or vibrate so as not to interrupt the group. Please do not answer calls/texts during group.
4. <u>Try it on.</u> Be willing to "try on" new ideas or ways of doing things that might not be what you prefer or are familiar with.
5. <u>Understand difference between intent and impact.</u> Try to understand and acknowledge impact. Denying the impact of something said by focusing on intent is often more destructive than the initial interaction.
6. <u>Practice self-focus.</u> Attend to and speak about your own experiences and responses. Do not speak for a whole group or express assumptions about the experience of others.

Copyright material from Monica M. Johnson and Michelle L. Melton (2021), *Addressing Race-Based Stress in Therapy with Black Clients*, Taylor & Francis

7. <u>Be mindful of your time</u>, so others can share. You have the "right to pass." You can say "I pass" if you don't wish to speak.
8. <u>Please no graphic/detailed accountings</u> of trauma experiences.

WORKSHEET 6.2

Defining Race and Racial Stress Handout

1. **A race is a socially defined grouping of humans based on (perceived) shared physical or social qualities into categories generally viewed as distinct.**

    While partially based on physical similarities within groups, science does not support that "race" has inherent physical or biological meaning. Race is regarded as a social construct, an identity which is assigned based on rules made by society.

2. **Racial stress describes chronically high levels of stress faced by members of minoritized groups.** Causes of racial stress are interpersonal experiences of racism, prejudice, and discrimination. Typical stress responses include high blood pressure, and anxiety and they build over time, eventually leading to poor mental and physical health.

3. **Race-based stress and traumatic stress is the consequence of emotional pain that a person may feel after encounters with racism or perceived discrimination.**

    It is important to understand that you can experience race-related stress even if you were mistaken that a racist act occurred. Race-related stress reactions only require that a person believes that they were the victim of racism.

Reflection Exercise

Recall one memorable racial encounter (vicarious or personal) and reflect on the questions below:

- Was it unexpected, out of control, emotionally painful?
- What were the reactions immediately after it happened?
- What are your reactions when thinking about the event now?
- Have you noticed any change in your behaviors since?

Copyright material from Monica M. Johnson and Michelle L. Melton (2021), *Addressing Race-Based Stress in Therapy with Black Clients*, Taylor & Francis

Session 2

Session 2 continues the focus on creating a shared language and community building through providing psychoeducation on types of racism. The activity and discussion will bridge the content from the first session and provide context for understanding racism as it exists in the current sociopolitical zeitgeist. After reviewing the handouts, create space for discussion and storytelling of lived experiences. During the discussion, be mindful of comments or stories that are not from the group members' experiences. Review the example below of a comment that focuses on others' experiences:

> Therapist: What are some examples of current racial injustices in our communities?
>
> Group Member A: Did you hear about the Black waiter whose White co-workers labeled his orders as "nigga orders?" You know they didn't fire those White workers. Just gave them a slap on the wrist and wrote them up! We can't even work without being reminded we are less than!
>
> Therapist: I'm wondering, as you're telling us about this event, can you say a bit more on how it impacts you personally? What does it mean in your daily life?

Now review the example below of a member comment that evidences self-focused sharing:

> Therapist: What are some examples of current racial injustices in our communities?
>
> Group Member A: Did you hear about the Black waiter whose White co-workers labeled his orders as "nigga orders?" You know they didn't fire those White workers. It's just another reminder that no matter what I do or where I go, White folks will always look down on me and I can do nothing about it ... because they will also be protected, and their behavior excused.

Notice that in the other-focused sharing, the therapist's follow-up question directed the conversation back to that member's personal thoughts or experiences. Use this technique to redirect conversation while validating the comments made.

As previously mentioned, storytelling is a powerful tool in creating community as well as increasing desensitization to the negative impact of racial stress and trauma. Be sure to engage in a mindfulness or relaxation practice of your choice to facilitate this process. When presenting the practice assignment, be sure review the instructions and to answer questions to provide clarity. Strongly encourage the members to complete the assignment before the next group, emphasizing its importance for healing racial traumas.

Session 2 Agenda and Activities

- Check-in
- Review content from previous session
- Handout: "Types of Racism" and "Microaggressions"
- Discussion/process/storytelling of experiences
- Mindfulness or relaxation exercise
- Review practice assignment: "Identifying Racial Microaggressions in Everyday Life"
- Wrap-up/summary

WORKSHEET 6.3

Types of Racism Handout

Racism builds on the (false) argument that one race is superior to other races. It refers to individual, cultural, institutional, and systemic ways by which different outcomes are created for different racial groups. The group historically or currently defined as White is advantaged, and groups historically or currently defined as non-White (African, Asian, Hispanic, Native American, etc.) are disadvantaged.

Individual	Institutional	Cultural
Individuals' beliefs, attitudes, and actions that support or perpetuate racism in conscious and unconscious ways. E.g. telling a racist joke, not hiring a person of color because "can't pronounce their name."	Ideologies and practices that seek to justify, or even cause, the unequal distribution of privileges or rights among groups that are social defined as racially or ethnically superior/inferior. E.g. the kinds of assets or sources of income that are considered in credit worthiness.	Representations, messages, and stories conveying the idea that behaviors and values associated with White people or "Whiteness" are automatically "better" or more "normal" than those associated with other racially defined groups. E.g. which facial features, hair types, and body types are considered beautiful.

Copyright material from Monica M. Johnson and Michelle L. Melton (2021), *Addressing Race-Based Stress in Therapy with Black Clients*, Taylor & Francis

Horizontal racism: negative attitudes and prejudice minority group members might have toward one another.

Internalized racism: how an individual from a marginalized group may incorporate into his or her own self-identity the dehumanizing messages of his or her own in-group made by others, and may denigrate his or her own in-group and act to distance himself or herself from members of that group.

Explicit racism: any speech or behaviors that demonstrate a conscious acknowledgment of racist attitudes and beliefs.

Implicit racism: unconscious biases, expectations, or tendencies that exist within an individual, regardless of ill-will or any self-aware prejudices.

WORKSHEET 6.4

Microaggressions Handout

- Verbal, non-verbal, and environmental slights, snubs, or insults directed toward persons based solely upon their minoritized group membership
- Pervasive and automatic in daily conversations and interactions such that they are often dismissed and glossed over as being innocent and innocuous
- *Micro-* refers the event, *not* the impact

There are three types of microaggressions:

1. *Microassaults*: explicit racial derogation characterized primarily by a verbal or nonverbal attack meant to hurt the intended victim.

    E.g. deliberately serving a White person before a person of color in a restaurant.

2. *Microinsults*: characterized by communications that convey rudeness and insensitivity and demean a person's racial heritage or identity, conveying a hidden insulting message to the person of color.

    E.g. employee "jokingly" asks the sole employee of color if she is the diversity hire.

3. *Microinvalidations*: communications that exclude, negate, or nullify the psychological thoughts, feelings, or experiential reality of a person of color.

    E.g. person of color being told that if they were nicer, more respectable, or more polite, people wouldn't discriminate against them.

Copyright material from Monica M. Johnson and Michelle L. Melton (2021), *Addressing Race-Based Stress in Therapy with Black Clients*, Taylor & Francis

Identifying Microaggressions

Read each example and determine what kind of microaggression is occurring.

Microaggression	Assault	Insult	Invalidation
1. "As a woman, I know what you go through as a racial minority."			
2. Person of color mistaken for a service worker.			
3. "When I look at you, I don't see color."			
4. A prime time television show only includes White characters.			
5. "Where are you really from?"			
6. A doctor's office waiting room with pictures displaying only White men, women, and children.			
7. "You're not like the rest of them."			
8. All hair care products for "ethnic hair" locked in a display case at the local store.			
9. "What are you?"			
10. "All lives matter."			

Copyright material from Monica M. Johnson and Michelle L. Melton (2021), *Addressing Race-Based Stress in Therapy with Black Clients*, Taylor & Francis

WORKSHEET 6.5

Identifying Racial Microaggressions in Everyday Life

Activity: Over the next seven days, keep a log of your encounters with microaggressions.

Encounter in which you notice (or even slightly suspect) microaggression

_____

_____

Description of scenario

_____

_____

Peak level of hurt/anger/frustration/distress/stress (1–10 scale); when, in relation to the encounter, did the peak emotion occur (instantaneously, seconds, minutes, hours, days)?

_____

_____

How did you react internally? (What kinds of thoughts when through your mind? What kinds of emotions did you feel? What kinds of physical responses/sensations were you able to detect e.g., increased heart rate, muscle tension, jaw clenching, perspiration, change in breathing?)

_____

_____

How did you respond externally?

_____

_____

Copyright material from Monica M. Johnson and Michelle L. Melton (2021), *Addressing Race-Based Stress in Therapy with Black Clients*, Taylor & Francis

How do you feel about your internal reaction?
_____
_____

How do you feel about your external response?
_____
_____

What level of hurt/anger/frustration/distress/stress do you feel now (1–10 scale)? If it is lower, what do you attribute this to?
_____
_____

Did you share this experience with anyone?
_____
_____

Session 3

Building upon the content and processes of the first and second sessions, Session 3 focuses on bringing awareness to the emotional and physiological impact of racial stress and trauma through psychoeducation and coping skill practice. Group members, then, are engaging in desensitization and reprocessing strategies to heal racial wounds.

Session 3 Agenda and Activities

- Check-in/practice assignment review
- Handout: "Common Emotional Responses to Racism"
- Discussion
- Review handout: "Finding a Healing Way"
  - Engage in practice of coping skills
- Review practice assignment: Coping skills/relaxation logs
- Wrap-up/summary

WORKSHEET 6.6

Common Emotional Responses to Racism Handout

- Stress is a state of mental or emotional strain or tension resulting from adverse or very demanding circumstances. The physical sensations of stress are our body's method of reacting to a condition such as a threat, challenge or physical and psychological barrier. This is our fight-flight-freeze response.
- Anxiety is a feeling of worry, nervousness, or unease, typically about an imminent event or something with an uncertain outcome. Anxiety is not always related to an underlying condition. It may be caused by stress that can result from work, school, personal relationships, etc.
- Every personal or vicarious encounter with racism contributes to a more insidious, chronic stress.
- A single experience of racism can bring to mind previous experiences with racism and awareness of longstanding history of racism directed toward similar others.
- Impact on mental and physical health:

Fear	Guilt
Hypervigilance	Feelings of loneliness
Headaches	Depression
Insomnia	Rage/Anger
Body aches	Diminished sense of well-being
Memory difficulty	Lowered life satisfaction
Self-blame	Decreased self-esteem
Confusion	Decreased self-compassion
Shame	Feeling hopeless
Feeling helpless	Thoughts of harming self/others

Copyright material from Monica M. Johnson and Michelle L. Melton (2021), *Addressing Race-Based Stress in Therapy with Black Clients*, Taylor & Francis

WORKSHEET 6.7

Finding a Healing Way Handout

Acknowledge. It is important to be aware and accept what you are feeling and experiencing. Start recognizing your anxious behavior and physical sensations in your body. Many of us perceive that anxiety is all in our heads, when in reality, it is also very much physical. These activities can increase your ability to identify the range of emotions and physical reactions you may be experiencing, all of which are normal and should not be discounted.

What to do to increase awareness:
- Journaling
- Mindful body scans for signs of stress/anxiety
- Actively reflect on your feelings

Discuss. Open discussion can help to minimize the tendency to internalize negative racial experiences, which can lead to feelings of anger, sadness, or anxiety. Speaking to others who may have similar reactions can also be normalizing and validating.

Engage in convversations:
- Talk to those that you trust (friends, family, confidantes, colleagues, and spiritual leaders)
- Speak on different experiences of hating and being hated
- Work at discovering links between experiences and among ourselves

Seek Support. Seeking guidance and support from others may help to facilitate positive coping and management of racial trauma responses.

Copyright material from Monica M. Johnson and Michelle L. Melton (2021), *Addressing Race-Based Stress in Therapy with Black Clients*, Taylor & Francis

People/places to seek support:

- Mental health professional (Employee Assistance Program, community agencies, etc)
- University health center
- Trusted mentors, spiritual leaders, or religious organizations and groups

Self-Care. The range of emotional and behavioral responses as a result of racial trauma requires proactive planning in order to begin the process of coping and healing. Self-care is a survival skill that promotes a balance between mental/physical rest and activity as well as social interaction. It must be deliberate and self-initiated.

Self-care activities that bring some pleasure and promote a healthy lifestyle to offset the effects of race-based stressors:

- Minimize intake of negative information, including social media outlets or discussions
- Internal coping strategies (mindfulness practices, meditation, reading, prayer, or other indigenous healing systems and faith practices)
- Activities that allow you to process your emotions externally (painting, drawing, spoken word recitations, singing, or dancing)
- Physical activities (exercising, going for walks, cooking, and sitting in outdoor spaces)

WORKSHEET 6.8

Coping Skill Practice Log

Practice the coping skills we learned in session today at least once a day. Write down each day and time that you practice. Also, rate your stress/distress *before* and *after* engaging in the skill. Use a scale from 1 to 10, with 10 being the most stress/distress you have ever felt and 1 being the most relaxed and calm you have ever felt. Bring this in with you to your next session.

Day:		*Stress Rating*	
Skill Used:		Before:	After:
Day:			
Skill Used:		Before:	After:
Day:			
Skill Used:		Before:	After:
Day:			
Skill Used:		Before:	After:
Day:			
Skill Used:		Before:	After:
Day:			
Skill Used:		Before:	After:
Day:			
Skill Used:		Before:	After:

Copyright material from Monica M. Johnson and Michelle L. Melton (2021), *Addressing Race-Based Stress in Therapy with Black Clients*, Taylor & Francis

Session 4

The fourth group session is designed to expand on the cognitive strategies from Session 3 by exploring internalized messages about Black racial identity/characteristics and empower group members to reform and or strengthen their racial identity. Facilitating discussion about identity will require flexibility on the therapist's part as group members may be at different stages of development. Your goal is not to "move" a group member's identity but allow for creative exploration. Additionally, you will acknowledge intersections of identity and how they shape a person's sense of self.

Session 4 Agenda and Activities

- Check-in/practice assignment review
- Explore the impact of racism and race-based stress on self-concept/identity
    - Handouts: "Racial Identity Development" and "Stages of Racial Identity Development (PoC)"
- Identify intersectional identities
    - Ask group members about their roles/identities and write on a whiteboard
        - Use ADDRESSING categories as a framework
- Discussion of intersecting identities on building resilience
    - What are the important intersections of your identities as a racial being?
    - How do these intersections relate to your power?
    - How do these intersections relate to your experience of oppression?
    - How do these intersections make you more resilient as a person?
    - What are you like when you are managing/responding to racism from your valued self?
- Wrap-up/summary

WORKSHEET 6.9

Racial Identity Development Handout

- Our understanding of ourselves develops over time and is influenced by our environment (caregivers, extended family, community, governance, etc.).
- Our racial identity is often shaped through distinct developmental moments that we cycle and recycle through.
- Our encounters with race and racism often mark these developmental moments.

1. Think back to a time before you knew about race and describe, in as much detail as possible, what you remember about those experiences.

   _____
   _____
   _____
   _____
   _____
   _____

2. When did you first realize you were a race? What happened? What did the experience teach you about your race?

   _____
   _____
   _____
   _____
   _____
   _____

Copyright material from Monica M. Johnson and Michelle L. Melton (2021), *Addressing Race-Based Stress in Therapy with Black Clients*, Taylor & Francis

3. What other discoveries have you made about your race since then?

   _____
   _____
   _____
   _____
   _____

4. What influence has racism had on your understanding of your own race?

   _____
   _____
   _____
   _____
   _____

WORKSHEET 6.10

Stages of Racial Identity Development (Poc) Handout

Conformity

- Oblivious to racism
- Ascribe to Whiteness (values, norms, behaviors)
- Marked by feelings of safety, contentment, satisfaction, comfort

Dissonance

- Experience negative racial event(s) (i.e. racism)
- Discover race preculdes you from benefits of White society
- Marked by feelings of confusion, anger, surprise, suspiciousness

Immersion

- Increased awarenes of racial inequities
- Increased distrust of White people and Whiteness
- Marked by feelings of anger, disillusionment, worry

Emersion

- Avoidance of contact with White people
- Greater need for contact with own racial group for comfort and validation
- Marked by feelings of anger, avoidance, comfort/connectedness

Internalization

- May experience positive interactions with White people
- Realization that racism is the problem versus specific groups of people

Copyright material from Monica M. Johnson and Michelle L. Melton (2021), *Addressing Race-Based Stress in Therapy with Black Clients*, Taylor & Francis

- Valuing own racial identity
- Marked by feelings of relief, curiosity

Integrative Awareness

- Positively identify with your own racial group while also acknowledging that other aspects of identity (gender, talents and abilities, unique experiences) contribute to their personhood
- Does not feel less than and able to reach out to other diverse groups to build community
- Marked by feelings of curiosity, openness, clarity, motivation, anger/anxiety

Discussion Questions

1. What stage of development reflects where you are currently?
2. What would you need or want to know to understand your racial identity in a more complete way?
3. What would you need or what to develop are positive and more complete sense of self?

Session 5

Session 5 continues the theme of reprocessing. The handout reviews internal coping strategies in response to negative racial encounters. The practice elements for the session are mindfulness and relaxation activities of your preference.

Session 5 Agenda and Activities

- Check-in/practice assignment review
- Handout: "Resilience in Response to Microaggressions"
- Self-regulation practices
  - Mind–body exercises
- Review practice assignment: coping skills/relaxation logs
- Wrap-up/summary

WORKSHEET 6.11

Resilience in Response to Microaggressions Handout

Resilience has been called the "ordinary magic" that you can use to bounce back from hard times. The best thing about resilience is that when you know how to tap into it, you can have an unlimited supply to draw from to navigate everyday challenges. Think of your own resilience as:

- Natural
- Something you can develop
- A set of skills you use to cope with adversity
- Developed within you and with others
- Composed of strategies and processes over time
- Multiplied, the more you develop it
- Connected to thriving in the future[1]

Activities to build resilience in response to negative racial encounters:

1. Name Microaggressions When They Happen
    - I just heard a microaggression
    - I just experienced a microaggression
    - I want to question myself now, but that was clearly a discriminatory/bigoted/racist remark
    - I was just treated poorly
    - This person would not have said that to a White person
2. Validate Your Feelings
    - Microaggressions happen quickly and can catch us off guard. Ask yourself "How do I feel about this statement or behavior?"

Copyright material from Monica M. Johnson and Michelle L. Melton (2021), *Addressing Race-Based Stress in Therapy with Black Clients*, Taylor & Francis

- Wide range of emotions can occur that can lead to numbness:
  - Anger: frustrated, aggressive, exasperated, disgusted, enraged
  - Fear: embarrassed, nervous, suspicious, frightened, terrified
  - Sadness: lonely, ashamed, depressed, hurt, disappointed
  - Numbness: disbelieving, withdrawn, shocked, indifferent
- Create a coping statement for validation:
  - "Because I just experienced [name the microaggression], it makes sense that I would feel [name and validate the emotion]"

Coping Statement/Affirmation:

_____

_____

Coping Statement/Affirmation:

_____

_____

3. Respond

   After naming and validating your experience, it is time to respond. This cCan entail either an internal response or external response:

   - Internal responses – includes thoughts or affirmations that reflect your value:
     - Thinking, "I am a valuable person"
     - Affirming yourself, "I do not deserve this treatment"
     - Acknowledging yourself, "I deserve to be treated respectfully and with dignity as a human being"

Copyright material from Monica M. Johnson and Michelle L. Melton (2021), *Addressing Race-Based Stress in Therapy with Black Clients*, Taylor & Francis

- External Responses – actions that include saying something to the person who committed the microaggression or include engaging in short-term or long-term protective behaviors in response:
    o Things to do:
        - Removing yourself from the situation
        - Seeking a safe place
        - Connecting with social supports
        - Engaging self-care activities, such as practicing mindfulness, reading, or listening to music, etc.
        - Journaling or blogging about your experience
        - Attending a support group or counseling

Session 6

Session 6 focuses on external coping strategies to address negative racial encounters, specifically microaggressions. The practice element for engaging in external responses to personal slights and snubs utilizes role plays and constructive feedback from observing group members. It is essential to facilitate discussion about fundamental risk (i.e. an elevated chance that certain aspirations and desires might not be obtainable, and heightened probability that basic needs, rights, and access to resources will be thwarted by circumstances beyond one's immediate control) and evaluate options for response when practicing external responses to microaggressions. For example, members should be encouraged to consider their physical safety when choosing to respond to racial encounters. In doing so, you are (1) acknowledging alternative responses to direct confrontation approaches, and (2) creating flexibility about how/when/if to respond. Creating this flexibility will likely decrease internalization of negative self-ruminations about one's capability to respond to racism in the moment.

Session 6 Agenda and Activities

- Check-in/practice assignment review
  - Handout: "Empowerment Responses to Racial Stress"
- Discussion/role plays
- Review practice assignment: write out additional responses
- Wrap-up/summary

WORKSHEET 6.12

Empowerment Responses to Racial Stress Handout

- The term *empowerment* refers to measures designed to increase the degree of autonomy and self-determination in individuals and communities to enable them to represent their interests in a responsible and self-determined way.
- It is the process of becoming *stronger and more confident*, especially in controlling one's life and claiming one's rights.
- Empowerment as action refers both to the *process* of self-empowerment to overcome any sense of powerlessness and lack of influence, and to recognize and use your resources.
- Various responses can be used to directly disarm or counteract the effects of microaggressions by challenging perpetrators.

Make the "Invisible" Visible
Neutralize the Microaggression
Educate the Offender
Seek External Reinforcement of Support

- Things to say:
  - "When you said ____, that wasn't respectful to who I am." (Describe what is happening)
  - "When you said ____, you assumed ____ about me." (Describe what is happening)
  - "When you said ____, I felt excluded." (Describe what is happening)
  - "You may not have realized it, but when you said ____, you weren't supportive of me." (Describe what is happening)
  - "Please don't say ____ to me again." (Describe what is happening)

Copyright material from Monica M. Johnson and Michelle L. Melton (2021), *Addressing Race-Based Stress in Therapy with Black Clients*, Taylor & Francis

- "Every time I come over, I find myself becoming uncomfortable because you make statements that I find offensive and hurtful." (Describe what is happening)
- "Whoa, let's not go there. Maybe we should focus on the task at hand." (interrupting and redirecting)
- "That behavior is against our code of conduct and could really get you in trouble." (Reminders about the rules)
- "Relax, I'm not dangerous." (Undermine the hidden message)

"In Your Own Words"

Make the "Invisible" Visible Statements:

1. _____
_____

2. _____
_____

Neutralize the Microaggression Statements:

1. _____
_____

2. _____
_____

Copyright material from Monica M. Johnson and Michelle L. Melton (2021), *Addressing Race-Based Stress in Therapy with Black Clients*, Taylor & Francis

Educate the Offender Statements:

1. _____
   _____
   _____

2. _____
   _____
   _____

Seek External Reinforcement of Support Options:

1. _____
   _____
   _____

2. _____
   _____
   _____

Session 7

Session 7 begins to consolidate the previous six sessions' tools and skills into a formal recovery plan. Additionally, focus is given to empowerment strategies to address macroaggressions through social action. Role plays, problem-solving, and SMART goal setting are tools to utilize during this session.

Session 7 Agenda and Activities

- Check-in/practice assignment review
- Handout: "Racial Wellness Toolbox"
- Discussion of each element (include coping skills practice)
  o Focus on social action and empowerment
- Review practice assignment: "Personal Commitment to Empowerment"
- Wrap-up/summary

WORKSHEET 6.13

Racial Wellness Toolbox Handout

Empowered Sense of Self	Describe what you are like when you are managing and responding to racism in a healthy manner: _____ _____ _____
Daily Maintenance of Centeredness in the Face of Racism	List connections or tools that help you maintain your centeredness in the face of racism (i.e. connect with friends who are equally or better able to engage in conversations about racial awareness; engage in prayer, spiritual practices, or use of mantras; engage in activism; and practice self- management, such as healthy eating, exercise, and favorite activities that help you feel centered). _____ _____ _____
Racial Stress Triggers and Response Plan	List items or experiences that tend to result in racial trauma symptoms (e.g., anger, isolation, sadness). After each item or experience identify a specific centeredness response (e.g., calling a friend, writing in your journal, activism). _____ _____ _____

Copyright material from Monica M. Johnson and Michelle L. Melton (2021), *Addressing Race-Based Stress in Therapy with Black Clients*, Taylor & Francis

Racial Trauma Early Warning Signs and Response Plan	List early warning signs that you are experiencing racial stress/trauma (e.g., body aches, fatigue, anxiety, depression, difficulty sleeping) and related ways of coping from your daily maintenance of centeredness coping skills list. _____ _____ _____
Acute Distress Response Plan	List signs that you are experiencing acute racial stress/trauma (e.g., hypervigilance and heightened emotional experiences, such as depression, anxiety, and anger, which compromise your ability to engage in chosen activities of work, sleep, or school). Identify an action plan for each item on your list. _____ _____ _____
Crisis Planning	Ask yourself how you would know if you were experiencing a crisis due to racism (e.g. thoughts of harm to others and/or self; inability to care for self and/or others; acute racial trauma symptoms that last longer than a specified duration). List a person(s) or additional resources to contact in the event you experience such a crisis. _____ _____ _____

Copyright material from Monica M. Johnson and Michelle L. Melton (2021), *Addressing Race-Based Stress in Therapy with Black Clients*, Taylor & Francis

| **Post-Crisis Planning** | List ways of reconnecting with yourself and your communities to regain centeredness in the face of racism. _____ _____ _____ |

Permissions granted by the authors for reproduction www.bc.edu/content/dam/files/schools/lsoe_sites/isprc/pdf/racialtraumaisrealManuscript.pdf

WORKSHEET 6.14

Personal Commitment to Empowerment

What can you personally do to create your vision of a more inclusive, racially equitable community/world?
  Some examples of personal commitments include:

- Attend community programming related to diversity issues
- Read a book or article, or watch a video on diversity/social justice
- Join an organization, campaign, or protest regarding social justice/restorative justice
- Create a community event on social justice

A 'personal commitment' means that I am willing to take several small steps to continue the process of positive change.
  Who can you discuss these issues with and follow-up on your commitments? Could you set up a time to meet or talk by phone?
  My accountability partner:

_____

What barriers might arise to following through on my commitments? How can I work around them?

Barriers	Workaround

Copyright material from Monica M. Johnson and Michelle L. Melton (2021), *Addressing Race-Based Stress in Therapy with Black Clients*, Taylor & Francis

Session 8

In the final session, group facilitators and members explicitly address the termination of the group. A good termination is an important final step in the group process. The tasks to complete include examining the impact of the group on each person, acknowledging the feelings about the group ending, providing an opportunity for giving and receiving feedback about the group experience and each member's role in it, exploring ways of carrying on what group members learned in the group, and allowing group members to process and discuss concerns about terminating. Considering your practice policy, you can also discuss next steps in treatment planning (i.e. referrals to additional mental health services, etc.). You can also provide community resources to continue the empowerment/social action plan members may create.

Terminating from the group may be difficult for some members, especially if they feel the group was the only place where they have been heard or validated about their racial experiences. It is important that you do not join in denying the ending of the group. Instead, help facilitate a "good goodbye." In doing so you honor the work and the relationships created.

Session 8 Agenda and Activities

- Check-in/practice assignment review
- Devise a handout called: "Community Events/Resources for Continued Empowerment"
- Tasks of termination
- Wrap-up/summary

References

Alcantara, C. & Gone, J.P. (2014). Multicultural issues in the clinical interview and diagnostic process. In F.T.L. Leong (Ed.), *APA Handbook of Multicultural Psychology: Applications and Training*. American Psychological Association.

American Counseling Association. (2014). *ACA code of ethics*. American Counseling Association.

American Nurses Association. (2015). *Code of ethics for nurses with interpretive statements*. American Nurses Association.

American Psychiatric Association. (2013a). *Diagnostic and statistical manual of mental disorders* (5th ed.). American Psychiatric Association.

American Psychiatric Association (2013b). *The principles of medical ethics with annotations especially applicable to psychiatry*. American Psychiatric Association.

American Psychological Association. (2017). *Ethical principles of psychologists and code of conduct*. American Psychological Association.

Atkins, R. (2014). Instruments measuring perceived racism/racial discrimination: Review and critique of factor analytic techniques. *International Journal of Health Service, 44*(4), 711–734.

Baca, L., & Smith, S. R. (2018). The role of self-reflection and self-assessment in the psychological assessment process. In S. R.

Smith, & R. Krishnamurthy (Eds.), *Diversity-sensitive personality assessment* (pp. 3–26). Routledge.

Beauchamp, T. L. (2014). The compatibility of universal morality, particular moralities, and multiculturalism. In W. Teays, J. S. Gordon, & A. D. Renteln (Eds.), *Global bioethics and human rights: Contemporary issues* (pp. 28–40). Rowman and Littlefield.

Bernard, H., Burlingame, G., Flores, P., Greene, L., Joyce, A., Kobos, J. C., … Feirman, D. (2008). Clinical practice guidelines for group psychotherapy. *International Journal of Group Psychotherapy, 58*(4), 455–542. https://doi.org/10.1521/ijgp.2008.58.4.455

Bhola, P., & Chaturvedi, S. K. (2017). Through a glass, darkly: Ethics of mental health practitioner-patient relationships in traditional societies. *International Journal of Culture and Mental Health, 10*(3), 285–297.

Bowen-Reid, T. L., & Harrell, J. P. (2002). Racist experiences and health incomes: An examination of spirituality as a buffer. *Journal of Black Psychology, 28*, 18–36. https://doi.org/10.1177/0095798402028001002

Bradford, L., Newkirk, C., & Holden, K. (2009). Stigma and mental health in African-Americans. In R. L. Braithwaite, S. E. Taylor, & H. M. Treadwell (Eds.), *Health issues in the Black community* (pp. 119–131). Jossey-Bass.

Brodsky, A. E., & Cattaneo, L. B. (2013). A Transconceptual model of empowerment and resilience: Divergence, convergence, and interactions in kindred community concepts. *American Journal of Community Psychology, 52*(3–4), 333–346.

Brown, L. (n.d.) Cultural competence. Retrieved from www.drlaurabrown.com/cultural-competence/

Bryant-Davis, T., & Ocampo, C. (2005). Racist incident-based trauma. *The Counseling Psychologist, 33*, 479–500. http://dx.doi.org/10.1177/0011000005276465

Bussing, R., & Gary, F. (2012). Eliminating mental health disparities by 2020: Everyone's actions matter. *Journal of the American Academy of Child & Adolescent Psychiatry, 51*(7), 663–666.

Carlson, M., Endlsey, M., Motley, D., Shawahin, L. N., & Williams, M. (2018). Addressing the impact of racism on Veterans of color:

A race-based stress and trauma intervention. *Psychology of Violence, 8*(6), 748–762. http://dx.doi.org/10.1037/vio0000221

Carter, R. T. (2007). Racism and psychological and emotional injury: Recognizing and assessing race-based traumatic stress. *The Counseling Psychologist, 35*(1), 13–105. https://doi.org/10.1177/0011000006292033

Carter, R. T., & Forsyth, J. M. (2009). A guide to the forensic assessment of race-based traumatic stress reactions. *Journal of the American Academy of Psychiatry and the Law, 37*, 28–40.

Carter, R. T., Johnson, V. E., Roberson, K., Mazzula, S. L., Kirkinis, K., & Sant-Barket, S. (2017). Race-based traumatic stress, racial identity statuses, and psychological functioning: An exploratory investigation. *Professional Psychology: Research and Practice, 48*(1), 30–37. https://doi.org/10.1037/pro0000116

Cimbora, D. M., & Krishnamurthy, R. (2018). Asking difficult questions: Client definitions. In S. R. Smith, & R. Krishnamurthy (Eds.), *Diversity-sensitive personality assessment* (pp. 27–42). Routledge.

Comas-Díaz, L. (2016). Racial trauma recovery: A race-informed therapeutic approach to racial wounds. In A. N. Alvarez, C. T. H. Liang, & H. A. Neville (Eds.), *The cost of racism for people of color: Contextualizing experiences of discrimination* (pp. 249–272). American Psychological Association. http://dx.doi.org/10.1037/14852-012

Comas-Díaz, L. (2000). An ethnopolitical approach to working with people of color. *American Psychologist, 55*(11), 1319–1325. https://doi.org/10.1037/0003-066X.55.11.1319

Cottone, R. R. (2004). Displacing the psychology of the individual in ethical decision-making: The social constructivism model. *Canadian Journal of Counseling, 38*(1), 5–13.

Cross, W. (1991). *Shades of Black: Diversity in African-American identity*. University Press.

DBT Research Updates. (n.d.). Retrieved from https://behavioraltech.org/research/updates/

DiAngelo, R. (2018). *White fragility: Why it's so hard for white people to talk about racism*. Beacon Press.

Durante, C. (2017). Bioethics and multiculturalism: Nuancing the discussion. *Journal of Medical Ethics, 44*(2), 77–83.

Epstein, R. M., & Hundert, E. M. (2002). Defining and assessing professional competence. *Journal of the American Medical Association, 287*(2), 226–235.

Ford, J. D., Fallot, R. D., & Harris, M. (2009). Group therapy. In C. A. Courtois, & J. D. Ford (Eds.), *Treating complex traumatic stress disorders: Evidenced-based guide* (pp. 415–440). Guildford Press.

Ford, M. P., & Hendrick, S. S. (2003). Therapists' sexual values for self and clients: Implications for practice and training. *Professional Psychology: Research and Practice, 34*(1), 80–87. http://dx.doi.org/10.1037/0735-7028.34.1.80

Forsyth, J., & Carter, R. T. (2012). The relationship between racial identity status attitudes, racism-related coping, and mental health among Black Americans. *Cultural Diversity and Ethnic Minority Psychology, 18*(2), 128–140. https://doi.org/10.1037/a0027660

Garcia, J. G., Cartwright, B., Winston, S. M., & Borzuchowska, B. (2003). A transcultural integrative model for ethical decision making in counseling. *Journal of Counseling & Development, 81*(3), 268–277. http://dx.doi.org/10.1002/j.1556-6678.2003.tb00253.x

Greppert, C. M. A., & Shelton, W. (2016). Health care ethics committees as mediators of social values and the culture of medicine. *AMA Journal of Ethics, 18*(5), 534–539.

Hammond, W. P. (2010). Psychosocial correlates of medical mistrust among African American men. *American Journal of Community Psychology, 45*, 87–106. 10.1007/s10464-009-9280-6

Harkness, K. L., Hayden, E. P., & Lopez-Duran, N. L. (2015). Stress sensitivity and stress sensitization in psychopathology: An introduction to the special section. *Journal of Abnormal Psychology, 124*(1), 1–3.

Harrell, J. P., Hall, S., & Taliaferro, J. (2003). Physiological responses to racism and discrimination: An assessment of the evidence. *American Journal of Public Health, 93*, 243–248.

Harries, B. (2014). We need to talk about race. *Sociology, 48*(6), 1107–1122. Retrieved from https://journals.sagepub.com/doi/full/10.1177/0038038514521714

Hays, P. A. (2001). *Addressing cultural complexities in practice: A framework for clinicians and counselors.* American Psychological Association.

Helms, J. E. (1996). Towards a methodology for measuring and assessing racial as distinguished from ethnic identity. In G. R. Sodowsky, & J. Impara (Eds.), *Multicultural assessment in counseling and clinical psychology* (pp. 143–192). Buros Institute of Mental Measurements.

Helms, J. E. (2008). *A race is a nice thing to have: A guide to being a White person or understanding the White persons in your life* (2nd ed.). Microtraining Associates.

Hiatt, J. M. (2006). *ADKAR: A model for change in business, government and our community.* Prosci Learning Center.

Holden, K., McGregor, B., Blanks, S., & Mahaffey, C. (2012). Psychosocial, socio-cultural, and environmental influences on mental help-seeking among African-American men. *Journal of Men's Health, 9*(2), 63–69. https://doi.org/10.1016/j.jomh.2012.03.002

Hook, J. N., Davis, D., Owen, J., & DeBlaere, C. (2017). *Cultural humility: Engaging diverse identities in therapy.* American Psychological Association. https://doi.org/10.1037/0000037-000

Hook, J. N., Davis, D. E., Owen, J., Worthington, E. L., Jr., & Utsey, S. O. (2013). Cultural humility: Measuring openness to culturally diverse clients. *Journal of Counseling Psychology, 60*(3), 353–366. https://doi.org/10.1037/a0032595

Hoop, J. G., DiPasquale, T., Hernandez, J. M., & Roberts, L. W. (2008). Ethics and culture in mental health care. *Journal of Ethics & Behavior, 18*(4), 353–372. https://doi.org/10.1080/10508420701713048

Hope in the Cities (n.d.). A call to community dialogue. Retrieved from www.hopeinthecities.org

Institute of Medicine. (2003). *Unequal treatment: Confronting racial and ethnic disparities in health care.* Washington, DC: The National Academies Press. https://doi.org/10.17226/10260

Kocet, M. M., & Herlihy, B. J. (2014). Addressing value-based conflicts within the counseling relationship: A decision-making model. *Journal of Counseling & Development, 92*(2), 180–186.

Kressin, N. R., Raymond, K. L., & Manze, M. (2008). Perceptions of race/ethnicity-based discrimination: A review of measures and evaluations of their usefulness for the health care setting. *Journal of Health Care for the Poor and Underserved, 19*(3), 697–730.

Linden, M. (2013). How to define, find and classify side effects in psychotherapy: From unwanted events to adverse treatment reactions. *Clinical Psychology and Psychotherapy, 20*(3), 286–296.

Linehan, M. M. (2015). *DBT® skills training handouts and worksheets* (2nd ed.). Guilford Press.

Louw, B. (2016). Cultural competence and ethical decision making for health care professionals. *Humanities and Social Sciences, 4*(2), 41. https://doi.org/10.11648/j.hss.s.2016040201.17 (ISSN: 2330-8184).

Matthews, A., Corrigan, P., Smith, B., & Aranda, F. (2006). A qualitative exploration of African-Americans' attitudes toward mental illness and mental illness treatment seeking. *Rehabilitation Education, 20*(4), 253–268.

Melton, M. L., Shrader, G., & Baca, L. (Summer, 2014). Professional identity development in black psychologists. *The Arizona Psychologist*, 11–15.

Murphy, C. (2015, August 14). Sex worker rights are human rights. Amnesty International Blog. Retrieved from www.amnesty.org/en/latest/news/2015/08/sex-workers-rights-arehuman-rights

National Association of Social Workers. (2017). *Code of ethics of the National Association of social workers*. National Association of Social Workers.

Office of Disease Prevention and Health Promotion. (n.d.). Mental health and mental health disorders. Retrieved from www.healthypeople.gov/2020/topics-objectives/topic/mental-health-and-mental-disorders

Owen, J., Drinane, J., Tao, K. W., Adelson, J. L., Hook, J. N., Davis, D., & Fookune, N. (2017). Racial/ethnic disparities in client unilateral termination: The role of therapists' cultural comfort. *Psychotherapy Research, 27*(1), 102–111. https://doi.org/10.1080/10503307.2015.1078517

Owen, J., Drinane, J. M., Tao, K. W., DasGupta, D. R., Zhang, Y., & Adelson, J. (2018). An experiemental test of microaggression detection in psychotherapy: Therapist multicultural orientation. *Professional Psychology, 49*(1), 9–21.

Owen, J., Imel, Z., Tao, K. W., Wampold, B., Smith, A., & Rodolfa, E. (2011). Cultural ruptures in short-term therapy: Working alliance as a mediator between clients' perceptions of microaggressions and therapy outcomes. *Counselling & Psychotherapy Research, 11*(3), 204–212. https://doi.org/10.1080/14733145.2010.491551

Owen, J., Tao, K. W., Drinane, J. M., Hook, J., Davis, D. E., & Kune, N. F. (2016). Client perceptions of therapists' multicultural orientation: Cultural (missed) opportunities and cultural humility. *Professional Psychology: Research and Practice, 47*(1), 30–37. https://doi.org/10.1037/pro0000046

Owen, J., Thomas, L., & Rodolfa, E. (2013). Stigma for seeking therapy: Self-stigma, social stigma, and therapeutic processes. *The Counseling Psychologist, 41*(6), 857–880. https://doi.org/10.1177/0011000012459365

Paasche-Orlow, M. (2004). The ethics of cultural competence. *Academic Medicine, 79*(4), 347–350.

Pieterse, A., Todd, N., Neville, & Carter, R. (2012). Perceived racism and mental health among black American adults: A meta-analytic review. *Journal of Counseling Psychology, 59*(1), 1–9. 10.1037/a0026208

Pieterse, A. L., & Carter, R. T. (2007). An examination of the relationship between general life stress, racism-related stress and psychological health among Black men. *Journal of Counseling Psychology, 54*, 101–109. https://doi.org/10.1037/0022-0167.54.1.101

Pope, K. S., Sonne, J. L., Greene, B. A., & Vasquez, M. J. (2006). *What therapists don't talk about and why: Understanding taboos that hurt us and our clients* (2nd ed.). American Psychological Association.

Rowe, M. (2008). Micro-affirmations and micro-inequities. *Journal of the International Ombudsman Association, 1*, 4548.

Rogers-Sirin, L., & Sirin, S. R. (2009). Cultural competence as an ethical requirement: Introducing a new educational model. *Journal of Diversity in Higher Education, 2*(1), 19–29.

Scott, L., McCoy, H., Munson, M., Snowden, L., & McMillen, J. (2011). Cultural mistrust of mental health professionals among black males transitioning from foster care. *Journal of Child and Family Studies, 20*(5), 605–613.

Shiles, M. (2009). Discriminatory referrals: Uncovering a potential ethical dilemma facing practitioners. *Ethics & Behavior, 19*, 142–155.

Soto, A., Smith, T. B., Griner, D., Rodriguez, M. D., & Bernal, G. (2019). Cultural adaptations and multicultural competence. In J. C. Norcross, & B. E. Wampold (Eds.), *Psychotherapy relationships that work: Volume 2: Evidenced-based therapist responsiveness* (3rd ed., pp. 86–132). Oxford University Press.

Substance Abuse and Mental Health Services Administration (2015). Racial/ethnic differences in mental health service use among adults. *HHS Publication No. SMA-15-4906*. Substance Abuse and Mental Health Services Administration.

Sue, D. W. (2010). *Microaggressions in everyday life: Race, gender, and sexual orientation.* John Wiley & Sons, Inc.

Sue, D. W. (2013). Race talk: The psychology of racial dialogues. *American Psychologist, 68*(8), 663–672. Retrieved from https://ncbi.nlm.nih.gov/pubmed/24320648

Sue, D. W. (2016). *Race talk and the conspiracy of silence: Understanding and facilitating difficult dialogues on race.* Wiley.

Sue, D. W., Alsaidi, S., Awad, M. N., Glaeser, E., Calle, C. Z., & Mendez, N. (2019). Disarming racial microaggressions: Microintervention strategies for targets, White allies, and bystanders. *American Psychologist, 74*(1), 128–142.

Sue, D. W., Bernier, J. E., Durran, A., Feinberg, L., Pedersen, P., Smith, E. J., & Vasquez-Nuttall, E. (1982). Position paper: Cross-cultural counseling competencies. *The Counseling Psychologist, 10*(2), 45–52.

Tandon, T., Armas-Cardona, G., & Grover, A. (2014). Sex work and trafficking: Can human rights lead us out of the impasse? *Health and Human Rights Journal*. Retrieved from http://www.hhrjournal.org/2014/10/21/sex-work-and-trafficking-can-human-rights-lead-us-out-of-the-impasse/ Accessed on 12/15/2019.

Tervalon, M., & Murray-Garcia, J. (1998). Cultural humility versus cultural competence: A critical distinction in defining physician training outcomes in multicultural education. *Journal of Health Care for the Poor and Underserved, 9*(2), 117–125.

Thomas, S. B., Fine, M. J., & Ibrahim, S. A. (2004). Health disparities: The importance of culture and health communication. *American Journal of Public Health, 94*(12), 2050.

Tinsley-Jones, H. A. (2001). Racism in our midst: Listening to psychologists of color. *Professional Psychology: Research and Practice, 32*(6), 573–580.

Toporek, R. L., & Williams, R. A. (2006). Ethics and professional issues related to the practice of social justice in counseling psychology. In R. L. Toporek, L. H. Gerstein, N. A. Fouad, G. Roysircar, & T. Israel (Eds.), *Handbook for social justice in counseling psychology: Leadership, vision, and action* (pp. 17–34). Sage.

Townes, D., Cunningham, N., & Chavez-Korell, S. (2009). Reexamining the relationships between racial identity, cultural mistrust, help-seeking attitudes, and preferences for black counselors. *Journal of Counseling Psychology, 56*(2), 330–336.

U.S. Department of Health and Human Services. (2001). *Mental health: Culture, race, and ethnicity—A supplement to mental health: A report of the surgeon general.* Substance Abuse and Mental Health Services Administration, Center for Mental Health Services, U.S. Department of Health and Human Services.

US Department of Health and Human Services. (2011). HHS action plan to reduce racial and ethnic health disparities: A nation free of disparities in health and health care. Retrieved from https://minorityhealth.hhs.gov/npa/files/plans/hhs/hhs_plan_complete.pdf

Utsey, S. O., Giesbrecht, N., Hook, J., & Stanard, P. M. (2008). Cultural, sociofamilial, and psychological resources that inhibit psychological distress in African Americans exposed to stressful life events and race-related stress. *Journal of Counseling Psychology, 55,* 49–62. https://doi.org/10.1037/0022-0167.55.1.49

Vandiver, B. J., Fhagen-Smith, P. E., Cokley, K. O., Cross, W. E., Jr., & Worrell, F. C. (2001). Cross's nigrescence model: From theory to scale to theory. *Journal of Multicultural Counseling and*

Development, 29(3), 174–200. https://doi.org/10.1002/j.2161-1912.2001.tb00516.x

Ward, E., Clark, L., & Heidrich, S. (2009). African American women's beliefs, coping behaviors, and barriers to seeking mental health services. *Qualitative Health Research, 11*, 1589–1601. https://doi.org/10.1177/1049732309350686

Wikipedia. (2019, November 19). Whataboutism https://en.wikipedia.org/wiki/Whataboutism

Williams, D., Neighbors, H., & Jackson, J. (2008). Racial/ethnic discrimination and health: Findings from community studies. *American Journal of Public Health, 98*(1), 29–37.

Williams, M. T., Metzger, I. W., Leins, C., & DeLapp, C. (2018). Assessing racial trauma within a DSM-5 framework: The UConn racial/ethnic stress and trauma survery. *Practice Innovations, 4*(4), 242–260.

Williams, M. T., Pena, A., & Mier-Chairez, J. (2017). Tools for assessing racism-related stress and trauma among Latinos. In L. T. Benuto (Ed.), *Toolkit for counseling spanish-speaking clients* (pp. 71–95). Springer International Publishing.

Index

page numbers in *italic* or **bold** type refer to figures and tables respectively.

acceptance skills (reality) 147–152
accumulating positives 126; in the Long Term (APL) 127, 128–130, 131; in the Short Term (APS) 127, 128
action urges 133, **135**, **136**
ADDRESSING framework 10–14, **11**, **12**, 22, 93–94, 107, 181
ADKAR model of change 47, 48
advocacy 47, 60–61; change models 47–53; empowerment of clients 131, 198, 199; identifying intervention strategies 53–58; implementing and assessing the advocacy plan 58–60; interview processes 66

affect *see* emotion
Affordable Care Act 54
alcohol 124
American Counseling Association's Code of Ethics (2014) 30
American Psychiatric Association's Principles of Medical Ethics (2010) 30
American Psychiatric Nurses Association Code of Ethics for Nurses (2015) 30
American Psychological Association: *Diagnostic and Statistical Manual of Mental Disorders* (5thed, 2013) *see* DSM-5; Ethical Principles and Code of Conduct for Psychologists (2017) 30, 33, 35–36, 44

APL (Accumulating Positives in the Long Term) 127, 128–130, 131
APS (Accumulating Positives in the Short Term) 127, 128
assessing race-based stress 65–66, 84; conceptual model 66, 72–74; DSM-5 criteria 74, 76–84; psychometrics of the (therapist's) self 66–71; tools 66, 74–76, 79, 80, 82
assimilation 14–15, 158, 184

BELIEF model 104–107, 111, 114
"be strong" attitude 112–113, 144
bias: addressing mental health disparities 54, 58, **59**; assessment instruments 66; cultural humility 6, 7; healthcare system 20; neutralizing 71, 84, 152; professional ethics 32, 34, 40, 41, 44, 45; race talk 114; self-reflection and the therapist's racial/cultural identity 14, 19, 28, 67, 69, 94, 97, 114
Black Awakening worksheet (1.2) 19, 23
black box paradigm 56
Bland, Sandra 162
blind spots *see* bias
BM *see* Build Mastery (BM)
bracketing (EB) 45
breathing techniques 119, 140

Brodsky, A. E. 47, 48
build mastery (BM) 127, 130–132, 134

CAP *see* cope ahead plan (CAP)
Carlson, M. 156
Carter, R. T. 14, 16, 17, 72, 73, 76, 77, 81
Cattaneo, L. B. 47, 48
CFI *see* Cultural Formation Interview (CFI)
change models 47–53
Cimbora, D. M. 67
codes of conduct 30–31, 32, 35–39, 44
Cognitive Processing Therapy (CPT) 108–109
colorblindness 17, 95
Comas-Díaz, L. 4, 17, 157, 158
Common Emotional Responses to Racism Handout (worksheet 6.6) 177
communication skills (client coping strategy) 130, 152–156, 158, 161
community building (group therapy) 158
confidentiality (group therapy) 160, 163, 164, 165
consultation: professional ethics 32, 40, 42, 44–45, 111; for self-reflection 5, 69, 71, 84, 92; *see also* advocacy
cope ahead plan (CAP) 118, 137–138, 149

Coping Skill Practice Log (worksheet 6.8) 180
CPT *see* Cognitive Processing Therapy (CPT)
Cross Model 14–17
cultural comfort 3, 6, 7, 54, **59**
cultural competence 3–4; assumptions of 4–6; interpersonal awareness and the ADDRESSING framework 9–14; multicultural orientation framework, components 3, 6–9; race talk 85; racial and professional identity 14–21, 23, 24–26, 114; *see also* professional ethics
Cultural Formation Interview (CFI) 66
cultural humility 3, 5, 6, 45, 54, 97, 99, 111
cultural opportunities 3, 6, 10, 97, 115
cultural racism 170
culture-specific barriers (access to mental health care) 47, 49–50, 55–56, 57, **59**, 60, 72

DBT *see* Dialectical Behavior Therapy (DBT)
DEAR MAN skills 152–153, 154
Defining Race and Racial Stress Handout (worksheet 6.2) 167

desensitization 157, 163, 169, 176
diagnosis 66, 67, 74, 76–84
Diagnostic and Statistical Manual of Mental Disorders (5th ed., American Psychiatric Association, 2013): Cultural Formation Interview (CFI) 66; diagnosis criteria 74, 76–84
Dialectical Behavior Therapy (DBT) 116–122, 123, 144, 147, 152–156; *see also* individual therapy interventions
DiAngelo, R. 59, 96
diet 123, 124
discriminatory harassment 73, 81
distraction skills 141–143
distress tolerance skills 138–140
DSM- 5: Cultural Formation Interview (CFI) 66; diagnosis criteria 74, 76–84

EB *see* ethical bracketing (EB)
Educate the Offender statements 191, 193
emersion *see* immersion-emersion
emotion: group race talk 161–162, 163, 188; individual regulation skills 72, 123–126, 127; responses to racism 176, 177; *see also* fear; guilt
emotion mind 117, 126, 133, 139

empowerment: advocacy and social action 58, 60, 61, 194, 198, 199; assessment 66, 74; change models 48, 49, 50, **51**, 52, 53; codes of conduct 47; individual interventions 131, 134, 137; Race-Based Stress and Resilience group (individual sessions) 163, 165, 181, 191, 192, 194, 195, 198; Race-Based Stress and Resilience group (overview) 157, 158–159, 160, 161; race talk 100–102
Empowerment Responses to Racial Stress Handout (worksheet 6.12) 191–193
EMPOWERment through distraction 141–143
Endlsey, M. 156
ethical bracketing (EB) 45
ethical practice *see* professional ethics
ethico-cultural decision-making model *see* Transcultural Integrative Model
exercise (physical) 123, 124, 125, 140, 179, 195
explicit racism 171, 172
external coping strategies 189, 190–193

fact checking 132–133, 134–135
faith practices 7, 125, 146, 149, 150, 179, 195
FAST skills 154, 156

fear: barriers to treatment 50, 55, 57; causing bias 71; of difference (race talk) 92, 108; as a response to racism 134, 135, 162, 177, 188
Finding a Healing Way Handout (worksheet 6.7) 178–179
Ford, M. P. 42
Forsyth, J. M. 72, 76, 77

gender **11**, 22, 34, 107
GIVE skills 152, 154, 156
goals: accumulating positives 127, 128, 129, 130; Build Mastery 130–131, 132; formal recovery planning 194; pre-group orientation 159, 160, 165; problem-solving 134, 137
Group Expectations and Agreements (worksheet 6.1) 165–166
group intervention 156; *see also* Race-Based Stress and Resilience (RSR) group
guilt 16, 18, 78, 135, 141, 177

healthcare systems: biomedical model 29–30; codes of conduct 30–31, 32, 35–39, 44; diagnosis 66, 67, 74, 76–84; Western-centricity 29, 66, 67; *see also* advocacy
Helms, J. E. 17–18
Hendrick, S. S. 42
Hiatt, J. M. 47, 48

Hook, J. N. 4, 5, 6, 71, 109
horizontal racism 171
household chores 131, 142
hypersensitivity 132–133

Identifying Racial Microaggressions in Everyday Life (worksheet 6.5) 174–175
identity *see* racial identity
immersion-emersion 15, 16, 17, 18, 184
implicit racism 171
improving the moment skills 141, 145–146
individual-level racism 170
individual therapy interventions 115–116; build mastery 127, 130–132; communication skills 152–156; coping ahead 137–138; distraction skills 141–143; distress tolerance skills 138–140; fact checking 132–133, 134–135; improving the moment skills 141, 145–146; mindfulness 116–122; opposite action 133–134, 135; PLEASE skill 123–125; problem solving 133, 134, 135, 137, 148; pros and cons 125–126; radical acceptance 147–152; self-soothing 131, 141, 144–145
initial assessment (group therapy) 159–160
institutionalized racism 85, 86

institutional racism 170
integrative awareness 185
internalization 16, 17, 70, 158, 171, 178, 181, 184–185, 190
intersectionality 107–108, 181
intervention strategies 72–73; *see also* individual therapy interventions; Race-Based Stress and Resilience (RSR) group

journaling 130, 131, 178

Krishnamurthy, R. 67

language *see* shared language
LGBTQIA community 83
Linehan, Marsha 118
logic mind 117–118

Make the "Invisible" Visible Statements 191, 192
marijuana 124
mastery building 127, 130–132, 134
MCO framework components *see* multicultural orientation framework components
MCRE *see* Model for Change Through Resilience and Empowerment (MCRE)
media consumption 134, 179
meditation 119, 125, 150, 151, 179
Mental Health: Culture, Race, and Ethnicity Report (2001) 54
mental health services *see* healthcare systems
microaffirmations 113, 114

microaggressions: assessment and diagnosis 75, 82, 83, 84; cultural humility and cultural opportunities 6–7; defined 91, 172; professional ethics 42; Race-Based Stress and Resilience (RSR) group techniques 161, 172–175, 186–189, 189, 190–193; and race talk in therapy 86–91, 91–92, 95–96, 110, 112–113, 114; strategic advocacy plan **59, 60**; techniques for individual therapy interventions 119, 121, 126, 137, 141

Microaggressions Handout (worksheet 6.4) 172–173

microassaults 172, 173

microinsults 172, 173

microinterventions 113, 114

microinvalidations 172, 173

mindfulness: being present 118, 120, 121–122; body scans 178; in group sessions 164, 186; radical acceptance 150; six skills 119–122, 128, 134, 139; three states of mind 116–118

mind, three states of 116–118

Model for Change Through Resilience and Empowerment (MCRE) 49–53, *50*, **51**

Motley, D. 156

multicultural orientation framework components 3, 6–9

muscle relaxation 140, 149

National Association of Social Workers (2017) 30

Neutralize the Microaggression Statements 191, 192

opposite action 133–134, 135, 136, 149–150, 151

Other Conditions That May Be a Focus of Clinical Attention (DSM category) 80, 81

Other Specified Trauma- and Stressor-Related Disorder (DSM category) 80–81, 82

OVERCOME (radical acceptance) 149–150

Owen, J. 3, 5, 6, 7, 91, 109

paced breathing 140

paired muscle relaxation 140

paternalism 57

PEDQ *see* Perceived Ethnic Discrimination Questionnaire (PEDQ)

Perceived Ethnic Discrimination Questionnaire (PEDQ) 75, 82

Personal Commitment to Empowerment (worksheet 6.14) 198

physical exercise 123, 124, 125, 140, 179, 195

pleasant events 127–128

PLEASE skill 123–125, 127

police 49–50, 52, 53, 67, 80, 122, 137

post-traumatic stress disorder (PTSD) 74, 76–77, 80, 82, 84

prayer 7, 125, 146, 149, 150, 179, 195
pre-screening (group therapy) 159–160
privilege: advocacy 57; assessing race-based stress 69; cultural competence 9–10, 13–14, 17, 18; fear of the police 68; race talk 85, 86, 96, 101, 113, 114; types of racism 170
problem solving 133, 134, 135, 137, 148, 152, 194
professional ethics 27–30, 46; ethico-cultural decision-making model *see* Transcultural Integrative Model; group therapy 160; value conflict management 42–46, 111
pros and cons emotion regulation skill 125–126
psychoeducaton 83–84, 157, 160, 161, 168, 176
psychometrics of the self 66–71

Race-Based Stress and Resilience (RSR) group 115, 157–163; session 1 (build community and create a shared language) 168–175; session 2 (types of racism and identifying microaggressions) 168–175; session 3 (awareness of emotional and physiological impact of racial stress and coping skill practice) 176–180; session 4 (racial identity) 181–185; session 5 (internal coping strategies) 186–189; session 6 (external coping strategies) 190–193; session 7 (formal recovery plan) 194–198; session 8 (group termination) 199
race talk 86; addressing cultural transgressions 112–113; assumptions 111, 112; being present in the therapy session 108–109; benefits of 92; client focused questions 99–101; colorblindness 95; cultural humility 5; group therapy sessions, defining race and racial stress (worksheet 6.2) 167; identify your own racial identity 97–99, 114; identity intersectionality acknowledgement 107–108; local community focused question 101–102; managing emotion in a group setting 161–162, 163, 188; and microaggression 86–91, 91–92, 95–96, 110, 112–113, 114; openness to new concepts and perspectives 109–111; race as a relevant topic 102–107; self-reflection 92–94, 97, 100–101, 108, 110,

114; shared language 72, 80, 85–86, 113–114, 157, 163, 168; value conflict 111; White fragility 96
racial identity: and cultural competence 19, 23, 24–26; development models of 14–18; ethical practice 28; group therapy session 4 181–185; internalized racism 158, 171, 181; intersectionality 107–108; openness to new concepts of 109–111; professional identity development 20–21; race talk 97–99, 114; and the requirement for an anti-racist stance 4; sociopolitical history 14
Racial Identity Development Handout (worksheet 6.9) 182–183
Racial Perceptions worksheet (1.3) 19, 24–26
"racial wellness toolbox" (worksheet 6.13) 194, 195–197
racism/racial discrimination and harassment, definitions of 73, 170–171
radical acceptance 147–152
reality acceptance skills 147–152
referring out 42; *see also* Transcultural Integrative Model
religion: cultural competence 4, 8, 9, **11**, **12**, 13, 22;

cultural-specific barriers to mental health care 56, 57; *see also* prayer
reprocessing 157, 176, 186
resilience: change models for advocacy 48, 49, **51**, 52–53, 61; group interventions 157, 158–159, 160, 165, 181, 186, 187–189; in identities 67, 111, 112
Resilience in Response to Microaggressions Handout (worksheet 6.11) 187–189
risk assessment (group therapy) 159, 162
role-play 190, 194
RSR *see* Race-Based Stress and Resilience (RSR) group

SAMHSA chartbook *see* Substance Abuse and Mental Health Services Administration (SAMHSA) chartbook (2015)
Seek External Reinforcement of Support Options 191, 193
self-care 179; *see also* PLEASE skill
self-esteem 53, 74, 78, 130, 177
self-love 144–145
self-reflection: cultural competence 5, 6, 10, 13–14, 19, 20, 22, 23; group therapy exercises 159, 163, 164, 167, 178; individual therapy interventions 130, 131; and professional ethics 32, 40,

43–44, 45; race talk 92–94, 97, 100–101, 108, 110, 114; for unbiased assessment/ diagnosis 67, 69–71, 84
self-soothing 131, 141, 144–145, 151–152
sexual orientation **11**, 14, 22
shame 18, 93, 94, 135, 177
shared language 72, 80, 85–86, 113–114, 157, 163, 168
Shawahin, L. N. 156
sleep: disturbance 7, 8, 78, 116, 124, 150, 196; PLEASE skill 123, 124, 125
social constructivism 31
Social Exclusion or Rejection (DSM category) 81, 82
socioeconomic status 10, **11**, 22, 107
Stages of Racial Identity Development (Poc) Handout (worksheet 6.10) 184–185
stereotypes 65, 110, 112, 152
STOP skill 139
storytelling of experiences 104, 147, 157, 158, 168, 169
strategic planning (advocacy and consultation) 53–60
stress sensitization hypothesis 77
stress vs. traumatic stress 72–73
Substance Abuse and Mental Health Services Administration (SAMHSA) chartbook (2015) 55
substance use 123, 124

Sue, D. W. 3, 59, 86, 91, 92, 95
supervision (professional) 42, 43, 44, 45, 46, 69, 84, 93
symptom clusters 74
systems-specific barriers (access to mental health care) 47, 54, 56, 58, 60

Target of (Perceived) Adverse Discrimination or Persecution (DSM category) 81
television 98–99, 106, 125, 127, 142, 173
temperature reduction 140
TIP skill 139–140
TMER *see* Transconceptual Model of Resilience and Empowerment
training: Dialectical Behavior Therapy (DBT) 116; race talk 86, 93, 94; self-evaluation 21, 70, 94; value conflict management 43, 44, 45, 46
Transconceptual Model of Resilience and Empowerment 47, 48–49
Transcultural Integrative Model: social constructivist approach 31; Step: 1: Interpreting the Situation Through Awareness and Fact Finding 32, 34–35; Step: 2: Formulating an Ethical Decision 32, 35–40; Step: 3: Weighing Competing Nonmoral

Values and Affirming the Course of Action 32, 40–41; Step: 4: Planning and Executing the Selected Course of Action 33, 41–42
transgender identification **11**, 83
traumatic stress: vs stress 72–73
Types of Racism Handout (worksheet 6.3) 170–171

Unequal Treatment Report (Institute of Medicine, 2003) 54
UnRESTS (University of Connecticut Racial/Ethnic Stress and Trauma Scale) 74–75, 79, 80, 82
values: Accumulating Positives in the Long Term (APL) 127, 128, 129, 130, 131; cultural competence 5, 6, 10, 14, 15; cultural mediation 15, 27–28, 170, 184; ethical conflict management 42–46, 111; FAST skills 154; healthcare systems 28, 29, 66, 67; logic mind 117; mindfulness skills 121; race talk 97, 100, 105, 109, 111, 112, 113; role in assessment 65, 67, 70; Transcultural Integrative Ethical Decision-Making Model 32, 35, 38, 40–41

volunteering 142

whataboutism 107
"When I first realized I was Black" (YouTube video) 163, 164
White fragility 96
White privilege: assessing race-based stress 69; and fear of the police 68; race talk 85, 86, 96, 113; racial identity development 17, 18, 184; types of racism 170
Williams, M. 156
wise mind 118, 126, 133, 135

YouTube video ("When I first realized I was Black") 163, 164

Milton Keynes UK
Ingram Content Group UK Ltd.
UKHW022035220924
448687UK00006B/29